THE
COMEBACK
COACH

JESSE BRAVERMAN

WITH GORDON F. SANDER

This book is dedicated to my mother and father, Midge and Harry Braverman, whose unqualified love and support was always there, to my brother Roger, my role model, to my wife Debbie, my best and most loyal friend, and to my coach, Joe Austin, my mentor and inspiration.

Note: Some names and identifying details in this book have been changed to protect the privacy of individuals.

The Comeback Coach shows the courage of Jesse to stand up for what he believed was right. A man of principle. He's a tribute to his family and mentor Joe Austin.

—Tony Macaluso, Coordinator for the Friends of Joe Austin

Jesse's career has touched the lives of hundreds of kids, but not before his commitment, talents and courage were tested to the breaking point by the self-interested machinations of school administrators, the frustrations of the legal system, and time in a purgatory not of his making. In the end, we find a man, vindicated and victorious, who has made his students and their parents better for having known him.

—David Homer, Retired Federal Judge

Being the father of three girls who had this man as their coach provided me with a somewhat different perspective from that of some of the other supporters or critics of Jesse Braverman. This is a story about the enduring lessons of getting back up when one is knocked down and the immutable truths that transcend sports. It's a triple play about perseverance, integrity, and giving of oneself to others. A man without children of his own unselfishly did for hundreds and hundreds of other people's children, ball players and special needs students alike, what someone, also unrelated to him, did for him when he was young. At least, that is who he always gave credit to besides his own parents. It may sound simple to say because it's what every parent can never do enough of for the ones they love, but Jesse just never, ever stopped saying, in spite of the bleakest circumstances or handicaps, "You can do this." Eventually, he almost always broke through.

—Peter J. Corrigan, Parent/Lawyer

Coach Braverman made the difficult team selection process civil and dignified, especially for those not selected. Every athlete was given a personal evaluation of their performance and a script of actions and encouragements to undertake and enhance their skills. Likewise, when the seasons ended, there would be long, very long "awards" celebrations. Each and every team member, regardless of their team stature or contribution to the W/L record, was recognized publicly for their positive influences on the team's successes as he saw them.

—Nancy McKenna, School Social Worker and Former Adirondack Director of the Empire State Games

CONTENTS

FOREWORD

By James Allen

THERE IS a power to the word "resilient" that always has fascinated me.

When I reflect upon the most tumultuous days in the life of Jesse Braverman, the word "resilient" certainly applies.

Braverman rebounded from the most difficult time in his life, yet that ascension was not rapid.

But to me, resiliency is not measured by a clock.

Braverman needed time to bounce back from having his ability to coach high school baseball—his passion—snatched away.

As a sportswriter for nearly thirty years, I first met Braverman during the early portion of my career and before he reached his crossroads in 1999.

I found him to be knowledgeable, devoted, and caring. He was someone who stood strong for the principles he truly believed in. Braverman would be put to the test upon becoming the varsity baseball coach at Bethlehem High School in 1995.

Before coaching a game, Braverman already had won a battle to land that position after the school's superintendent attempted to circumvent the rules and appoint the candidate he desired.

Even as he quickly began to achieve success guiding his high school team, Braverman was about to discover his passion to coach would have parameters placed upon it.

Braverman had coached the freshman baseball team for ten years prior to being appointed varsity coach. In 1987, two years after he began as freshman coach, Braverman created the summertime Bethlehem Mickey Mantle team for kids ages fifteen and sixteen. At that time, there was a New York State rule prohibiting coaches from coaching out of season, and school officials were aware of Braverman's creation of the Mickey Mantle team, but nothing was said to him.

The Suburban Council, the league of which Bethlehem is a member, then enacted in 1997 a similar rule prohibiting coaches from working with 50 percent of would-be varsity players during the summer. Some of the players Braverman coached during summer would become his varsity players, but not all.

The league rule was put in place to prevent coaches from applying undo pressure upon varsity athletes to compete outside high school. While the general concept of the rule was well-intentioned, it also was vague, flawed, and readily abused.

Immediately after the rule was put into effect, Braverman, then varsity coach, was told to stop coaching during the summer.

Braverman eventually was issued a professional ultimatum: Give up summer coaching and keep your job, or keep coaching the summer team and lose the varsity job.

Braverman refused to take the easy road. He wasn't attempting to gain any competitive advantage or show disrespect. He merely wanted to give kids in his area the chance to play summer baseball and be involved in the coaching.

Braverman knew he was being unfairly singled out and why it was happening. He was not shocked the league he coached in—and the power brokers inside its structure—wanted to make an example out of him.

Even though Braverman understood the scope of what was about to happen, it did not soften the sting and magnitude of feeling wronged after he was eventually forced out as varsity coach and later lost a lawsuit against the league and his school.

That pain nearly consumed him.

But anyone who knows Jesse Braverman realizes he is not a quitter.

He eventually got another chance to coach high school baseball at La Salle Institute. He was back again doing what he loved most.

Braverman told me after leading La Salle to a second sectional title in 2008, "When people show faith in you, you want to give something back."

As you will soon read in *Comeback Coach*, Braverman has given back plenty.

The way I view Jesse Braverman is direct and simple: He coaches life and teaches baseball, not the other way around.

Baseball is his passion. The sport has provided him a canvas to create great beauty.

Sure, Braverman's players learned how to play baseball properly, acquired the same love for the sport and all its complexities their coach carries, and scraped to succeed.

Yet more than anything, Braverman's players learned about life from a resilient man who refused to give in.

ACKNOWLEDGEMENTS

COMPLETING a book, as I have learned, is not a sprint, but a marathon. It requires endurance and perseverance that are both physical and mental. Numerous people have given me the support, encouragement, and assistance that have enabled me to complete this project.

No one was more indispensable to *The Comeback Coach* than my coauthor, Gordon F. Sander. He was vital to all aspects of the project, including inception, writing, staff creation and guidance, photography, and production.

Gordon spent a total of between two and two and a half years over a ten-year period working on this book, or approximately one-quarter of his time during the decade. He took between twenty-five and thirty meetings of three to five hours, either in Albany or in Ithaca. For this purpose, he often spent between six and ten hours traveling by uncomfortable long-distance bus to and from Albany for on-site meetings, for which he often had to endure long stopovers in Syracuse or Binghamton, frequently arriving back in Ithaca after midnight.

When Gordon and I were reunited thirty-five years after our childhood friendship, he encouraged me to express my feelings of despair in writing. Five years later, Gordon read my sometimes garbled and incoherent original manuscript numerous times in order to get a handle on the project. He then proceeded to conceive and outline the twelve-chapter book. Finally, Gordon wrote, rewrote, and rewrote again, the two-hundred-page manuscript you see here.

There was a lot more to this book than just the writing. Gordon took the initiative of doing extensive research on baseball and special education. He conducted email interviews with several of my friends and colleagues. In addition, he visited Attica State Correctional Facility with me in order to better understand my former student John, who is the subject of chapter 8. Later, he contributed his considerable photography skills, caption writing, cover design, and jacket copy. Throughout all of this, he often kept our teetering effort afloat with his irrepressible sense of humor.

A project of this scope requires the contributions and expertise of a competent staff. Gordon single-handedly arranged for and guided this assistance. He enlisted the help of former Cornell assistant Scott Reu to construct a website for the book. He recruited another former assistant from Finland, Mau Vuori, to outline the original manuscript in order to adapt it into credible form. Perhaps the catalyst for bringing the project to fruition occurred when Gordon suggested and successfully brought on board another former editorial assistant at Cornell, Sarah Ruth Jacobs, to serve as editor-cum-manager. Over the course of their fruitful six-month collaboration, Gordon and Sarah met numerous times as well as exchanged hundreds of texts and emails.

Thank you for everything, Gordon!

I am most grateful to my mother and father, Mildred and Harry Braverman, whose unqualified love and unselfish guidance helped me endure life's challenges and provided me a strong foundation on which to build. I also thank my brother Roger for being a model of dedication and self-discipline, some of which thankfully rubbed off on me.

I have been blessed with the ideal co-pilot for my lifetime journey in my wife Debbie. I am certain that not only those who have participated in sports, but also those who have merely lived in this world, are familiar with the concept of a "fair weather fan." There is no way this journey would have reached this destination or the future ones to come if Debbie had been a "fair weather fan."

How does one acknowledge a person like my childhood coach Joe Austin? How does one use words to represent the significance of such a man to one's life? Mario Cuomo, former

Governor of New York State and an Austin disciple himself, called him "the most important man in my life after my father." Joe taught me about baseball and life, not necessarily in that order. He will forever be my mentor and my inspiration.

The members of the Pavlovich family, including the late Lou Sr., Lou Jr., and Diane, have proven the adage, "A friend in need is a friend indeed." Through their publication, *Collegiate Baseball Newspaper*, they threw me a lifeline and championed my cause while I was in coaching exile and trapped in the Long Tunnel, the term I use to describe that difficult period. It is my privilege to have them as friends.

I don't know where I would be without my lifelong friends. In today's ever-shifting world, it has become all too rare to see relationships stand the test of time, and yet, I have been most fortunate to have close friendships that have lasted from four to six decades. Bill Rappaport, the late Jimmy Gonedes, Bruce Lerro, Bobby Sacca, Peter Lord, Stu Frankel, John Brennan, and Mark Band have my sincere appreciation and perpetual loyalty. I would also like to acknowledge my mother's dear friend, the late Claire Inselman, who took me into her home during Midge's illness in 1959.

During my thirty-two-year teaching career at the Bethlehem Middle School I had the opportunity to learn from master teachers such as Diane Wallace, Donna Varriale, the late Lois Mannheimer, and Jane Cappiello. I also received expert guidance from Principals Fred Burdick and Stephen Lobban; Assistant Principal, the late George Stagnitta; and Special Education Supervisor and School Psychologist, the late Clarence Spain.

I have always considered myself to be a teacher first. After all, every coach is a teacher, though not all teachers are coaches. As a teacher, my greatest concern has been the social, emotional, and educational well-being of my students. Throughout my forty-four years in education I thank my students for generally demonstrating effort, courage, and determination and for being a pleasure to work with. I have frequently felt proud of the adults they have become.

Thanks, too, to my coaching colleagues for mentoring me along the way, especially Nelson Harrington, Bob Salamone, Ken Hodge, Kim Wise, and Vicki Bylsma. Special thanks to Athletic Directors Ray Sliter and Pat Mulcahy for their faith in me, which I hope I have justified.

So much of whatever success I have enjoyed in coaching is attributable to the numerous assistant coaches who have worked alongside me. I thank each and every one of you. The list of extraordinary student-athletes I have had the privilege of coaching is even longer. A special note of appreciation is extended to my undefeated 1992-93 freshman girls basketball team who not only excelled on the court, but in the classroom as well. My life has been enriched by our shared experience.

It was not easy for me to endure the despair that I felt at Bethlehem after I was dismissed. The numerous people whose support helped me see the light included Matt Quatraro; Pat Hughes; Peter Corrigan; Jim Carriero; Nancy McKenna; Mary, Brad, and Kyle Snyder; Larry, Sandi, and Alex Hackman; Jim Kelly; Cory Czajka; Phoebe Smith; Ken and Norm Hayner; Bill and Karen Tierney; and Karl Steffen.

When my world was at its bleakest, along came La Salle Institute. There is an uncommon integrity and genuineness about this school. In today's high school sports, coaches cannot survive without administrative support, and at La Salle that support is always there. In fact, the atmosphere at the school is one that you would see in a family. When Debbie had to undergo heart surgery in 2007, the baseball families took turns bringing dinner to our house when she first came home from the hospital. Who would believe that a Jewish kid from Queens could be the baseball coach at a Catholic school, but it's true, and I absolutely love it!

Several other friends provided valuable assistance. Roger Widmann encouraged Gordon to complete the project at a time when his interest was waning and very well may have made the difference in re-energizing my talented coauthor. Frank Saragaglia invited me to assist him in coaching a community women's basketball team at a time when I needed it most. Former

Bethlehem colleague Steve Rider understood my plight like few others could and his companionship was most welcome. Coaches Rob Helm, Rick Leach, and Todd Hayes worked with me on the field and court and helped ease me back to my old self. Jeff Pesnel, as a member of the Bethlehem community, reached out to me in my time of need. Former Bethlehem baseball players Ted Hartman, Nathanial Sajdak, Kevin Blanchard, Josh Naylor, Chris Gerber, Josh Formica, and Jason Colacino reminded me that maybe my life still had meaning after all.

A very special thanks is extended to designer Tim Nerney whose dedication and creativity produced an attractive and inspirational cover for the book. My appreciation also goes to illustrator Justin Schafer whose rendition of me captures the theme of the story.

A couple of years ago, the son of one my closest friends said to me, "No offense, but who is going to be interested in a book about you?" I had to admit this was a valid question. Therefore, it would be difficult to overstate the contributions of David Doyle and Charles Wiff from Gramercy Communications. They have worked tirelessly and skillfully to market *The Comeback Coach* and find the widest possible audience.

I offer a special thanks to my editor, Sarah Ruth Jacobs, who skillfully and patiently improved the manuscript, assisted with all aspects of the book's production, and guided us across the finish line.

JB
Glenmont, New York
October 2017

PROLOGUE:
THE GAME

A MOMENT to remember from a coach's life.

I certainly remember it.

Time: a few minutes before one in the morning.

Date: June 7, 2008.

Place: Joe Bruno Stadium, Troy, New York.

The game: the New York State Section II Class AA championship game between the Cadets of La Salle Institute, a Catholic school located in Troy, and the Columbia Blue Devils.

Inning: the top of the seventh.

The score: tied, 2 – 2.

Attendance: 4,264 rabid La Salle and Columbia fans.

That's the scene. Now let's zoom in on the La Salle dugout, where the Cadets, in their now well-soiled blue uniforms, are gathered on the top step, anxiously watching the action along with their coach, Jesse Braverman, a tightly coiled man of fifty-seven. At the moment, the Blue Devils have two runners on base, including the potential go-ahead run, on first and second.

The game, the fifth sectional championship game to be played that evening, and which only began after a thunderstorm, is by far the latest game the Cadets have played this season—or any other recent season, for that matter. The Cadets' star pitcher, a strapping fifteen year old sophomore by the name of David Roseboom, has pitched a magnificent game thus far.

Now, however, he is clearly tiring. After retiring the first batter, Roseboom has given up back-to-back walks to the Devils. With one of the Devils' most dangerous hitters, center fielder Pat Puentes, due up, the momentum of the game—that critical, intangible thing—seems to be tilting toward the Blue Devils. The eyes of hundreds of La Salle fans are fixed on Roseboom, trying to will the flagging pitcher the strength to power through the crisis and keep the game even as the lanky Puentes steps up to the plate.

Coach Braverman's eyes, however, are fixed on those of the lead runner, the aggressive Matt Montross, who is taking a healthy lead off second base, as well as those of Chris Dedrick, the Devils' formidable coach, who is standing in the third base coach box. Further zooming in, Braverman, who has 20/20 eyesight—and an even better baseball antenna—detects what he later calls "unusual eye contact" between Montross and Dedrick, who is trying to look as casual as possible. However Montross's darting eyes give him away.

Time to bushwhack the bushwhacker. Quickly, Braverman gives his ace the pickoff signal. Successfully picking off a runner from second base is a tricky maneuver for any pitcher, no less a fifteen-year-old high school hurler, but Braverman has put Roseboom through his paces well. A one-time high school star pitcher himself, Braverman has spent myriad hours in practice with Roseboom and the other La Salle pitchers, demonstrating how, in order to take advantage of a potential pickoff situation, a pitcher needs to first raise his front leg with his head looking directly at the batter while exhibiting no change in his normal posture as he delivers the pitch so as not to telegraph *his* intentions, *then* when his front knee is at its apex, quickly pirouette around and run directly at the prospective thief, trapping him between the bases, before either tagging him himself or tossing it to his third baseman and permitting him to do the honors.

It's a beautiful move when executed properly, something out of modern dance really, and tonight it is indeed executed beautifully, just as practiced. Roseboom feints, spins, and runs directly at the flustered Montross, before tossing the ball to La Salle third baseman Kyle Charron, who tags him out with a resounding *thwack!*

As the La Salle bench—along with their charged-up fans—*erupts* into startled cheers at the surprise pickoff, Braverman allows himself a small private smile. The game isn't over; not by a long shot. But something has changed; the players, as well as the fans, sense this too, a subtle, almost subliminal yet palpable feeling that the balance of the contest has altered, that the gods of baseball have crossed the diamond and lined up on La Salle's side. This feeling is confirmed on the very next pitch, when the revivified Roseboom, responding to a brilliant call by his catcher, Lukas Bridenbeck, fires a fastball down the middle and strikes out Puentes, leaving the toughest out of the Devils' lineup, Nolan Gaige, in the on-deck circle. New game now. More cheers…

****

THE GAME continues. The clock is nearing one a.m. now. Still nary a yawn in sight.

Bottom of the seventh now. The score is still tied, 2 – 2. Undeniably, the momentum is with La Salle now, but as Braverman knows—as everyone who is watching knows—that can change in an instant. Time to score; time to close the deal. Next up: La Salle's determined left fielder, Brian Beaury. Braverman feels good about Beaury leading off because he is a patient hitter with a good eye who has led the Cadets in walks over the past season. On the other hand, Columbia's fireballer, Nolan Gaige, gives no indication of tiring. The duel is on. Gaige uncorks. The crowd of four thousand plus holds its collective breath.

Three quick pitches later the count stands at one and two. Looks like Beaury is going to be out of there pretty soon. But no, wait. Gaige calmly fires another fastball right down the middle, and Beaury just as calmly fires a bazooka shot up the middle for a clean single. The Cadets have their leadoff man on. Dedrick, the Columbia coach, decides to make a pitching change. He signals for his ace pitcher, Austin Chase, to come in to replace Gaige, who, with a shrug, and a nod to his steadfast fans in the stands, trots out to left field. In case the Devils survive the inning

Dedrick wants Gaige's powerful bat to remain in the batting order.

Normally in this situation, Braverman would have the next batter, Lukas Bridenbeck, who is an excellent bunter, sacrifice Beaury to second. But the Cadet catcher looks uncomfortable on his first attempt so instead Braverman lets Bridenbeck swing away, whereupon the disappointed youngster proceeds to fly out.

Braverman quickly recalculates. The momentum is shifting again; the wheel spring that had been swinging in La Salle's favor has suddenly stopped. As the next batter, Cadet second baseman Will Remillard, steps into the box, the coach knows what he is going to do. By the time Chase is ready to throw, he has made his decision; he is going to let Beaury steal. It's a risk because if Beaury is thrown out, La Salle will be down to its last out. However, as Braverman knows from his detailed scouting report, the Columbia catcher, Ian Bridegroom, has a strong arm but is sometimes inconsistent. Too, it will be a little easier to get a jump off Chase, a tall right-handed pitcher with a good breaking ball, which he will likely use against a good hitter like Remillard. Quickly, imperceptibly, Braverman gives the sign to Beaury to steal. Then he goes back to his routine of idly kicking stones.

The game, the twenty-eight hundredth some odd game of Braverman's thirty-year-long high school coaching career, continues.

No dunce himself, Dedrick correctly guesses that Beaury is going to steal and calls for Chase to pitch out. He does so. Bridegroom duly jumps to the side and fires to second base. However, as Braverman hoped, his throw is off, way off, leaving a grinning Beaury safe at second. Beaury could stay there. He doesn't. He is an aggressive baserunner, and true to form, he seizes the moment.

As his coach proudly watches on, the fearless left fielder keeps on going, streaking for third. He makes it. More cheers from the La Salle fans. The pendulum is really swinging La Salle's way now.

Dedrick, now in emergency mode, pulls his infield in as the Cadet second baseman, Will Remillard, steps into the batter's box. For a moment, as he later recounts, Braverman considers calling for a suicide squeeze, another La Salle specialty. But all he needs to do is to take one look at the determined Remillard to know what he is going to do. Braverman decides to let him take his swing and goes back to kicking stones.

A moment—a long moment—later, Chase wheels and fires a curveball down the middle at Remillard. Remillard responds with his own lightning, sending the pitch through the box and into center field as his teammate, Beaury, trots home with the winning run. Game to La Salle; championship to La Salle. On the field bedlam breaks out as the exultant La Salle players fall into the familiar victory scrum, where they are soon joined by some equally ecstatic civilian Cadets. Someone—it looks like Roseboom, hard to tell in that hysterical mass—hauls Braverman onto his shoulders; the victorious team walks off.

The time: *who cares?*

****

A HALF HOUR later, a beaming Braverman, his thrilled wife Deb, and myself make our way out of the stadium to the coach's car. Braverman prides himself on not gloating, but on this night, this special night, he can't contain his pride in the team and their collective achievement. *"Did you see that pick off!"* he exclaims, giddily.

Did you see that pick off?

For me, a lost childhood friend who had only reconnected with Braverman several years before, and who is now helping him write a book about his incredible life story, the moment seems like an apotheosis. It is hard for me to believe that this is the same man who, several years before, having just been dismissed as coach of his first championship team after a long, bizarre bureaucratic struggle straight out of Kafka, had been the very picture of gloom.

Who said that there are no second acts in American lives?

Did you see that pick off?

And what a second act Jesse Braverman's Act II has been. Something out of Hollywood, really. "The Braverman

Redemption" sportswriter James Allen of the *Albany Times Union* has called it.

But first, let's learn a little more about the first, long, alternately triumphant and tragic act. For Jesse Braverman has had an extraordinary life, and career, indeed.

Indeed, one for the books, one might say.

Gordon F. Sander

CHAPTER 1:
THE CANDY STORE

THE BETTER part of my first eighteen years of life revolved around a series of two small candy stores in Queens, New York. It was there that I learned about the value of hard work, the importance of family, and the fundamentals of business, including the Darwinian nature of the American enterprise. It was there that I learned, read about, and discussed the major events of my childhood, including the race to space, the civil rights struggle, the assassination of John F. Kennedy, and the highs and lows of the then seemingly perpetual world champion New York Yankees, alongside my parents, Harry and Midge Braverman, my brother, Roger, and our customers.

It's also where I learned how to make an egg cream, and where my personal concoction of this uniquely New York drink actually became a hit with our customers. To be sure, in a way, you could say that those two Queens, New York candy stores were, collectively, my first classroom.

Before I proceed any further, perhaps I had better elaborate on what I actually mean by a candy store, i.e., a New York—or should I say, a New *Yawk*—candy store, because unless you grew up in mid-century New York City, you probably will have no idea of what I mean.

Like such bygone accoutrements of New York life as the Manhattan elevated train and *The New York Herald Tribune*, the New York candy store of the kind I grew up in, and the casual, unhurried, mutually caring way of life which it represented, and of which it was a fulcrum, is largely gone with the wind—or should I say, gone with the Internet.

And what a shame that is. Because for a time, a very special time, from the Depression, when my parents grew up, until the 1970s, when I went off to college and began my dual career as a special education teacher and an athletic coach, virtually every New York City neighborhood had one.

****

ESSENTIALLY, the term candy store is something of a misnomer. Of course, the old-style New York candy store dispensed all kinds of hard and soft candy, gum, milkshakes, and, of course, egg creams in all of their delectable and mouthwatering varieties. In this sense, they resembled the old-fashioned ice cream fountains of the nineteenth and early twentieth centuries.

But that was only the start—the first scoop, so to speak.

In addition to being a candy store and ice cream fountain, the typical New York candy store was also a tobacconist dispensing all manner of tobacco products, including cigars and pipe tobacco, for the close to half of the American population who chose to partake of those products in those pre-Surgeon General's warning, smoke-enfurled, days.

Additionally, the neighborhood candy store also functioned as a stationer and was crammed with notebooks, notepads, pens and pencils, and erasers, for the back-to-school crowd, as well as greeting cards for all occasions and denominations.

It also was a toy and sporting goods store, albeit of the most rudimentary kind, selling Spaldings and Pensy Pinkies, the latter of which was the brand name of the most bouncy form of rubber balls, and thick stickball bats for the neighborhood kids who played that quintessential sport, stickball,[1] as well as Revell model sets for the young, vicarious naval warfare crowd.

---

[1] *Stickball* is a peculiarly New York version of baseball played with a long thin bat, a rubber ball, and between two and six people. In the Queens version, the strike zone is painted on a wall.

It also was a newsagent, where every day locals could get their copies of *The New York Times, The New York Daily News, The New York Post, The World Telegram, The New York Mirror, The Herald Tribune, The Long Island Star Journal,* and *The Long Island Press*—or, as often used to be the case, one of several of the cornucopia of newspapers published in New York in the pre-Internet era, and which, at least up until the 1960s, were the primary means for New Yorkers to get their daily news fix. Candy stores also sold magazines and well-stocked racks of paperback books, mostly of the thriller kind.

Finally, and above and beyond all of that, the candy store often also served as a kind of community center, where the residents of the neighborhood—usually from the same block and the next one, for more likely than not, there was another similar store two or three blocks over--could talk, gossip, and commiserate, or all three. Purchase was not required, but civil behavior *was*. Perhaps the closest analogy would be the small town general store— except, of course, that the candy store was located in New York City.

Acting as surrogate bartenders to the abstaining public of all ages and serving as head proctors of this classroom in life was the hard-working, endearing couple who owned the establishment, also known as Mom and Pop. Oftentimes, one or more of the couple's kids would be helping out with the chores, pulling sodas, discussing the comparative merits of this or that candy with the younger clientele, and supplying ready smiles when their parents were too weary from their dawn-to-dusk duties.

I should know, because in my case, the long-suffering Mom and Pop behind the counter of the two Queens candy stores, one in Jamaica, the other in Flushing, that I grew up in, were *my* mother and father, Midge and Harry Braverman, and the kid with the New York Yankees cap and ready smile who was helping them out and learning about the peculiarities of candy store economics and life was me.

It was those stores, both known as Harry and Midge's, after my father and mother, that served as both the backdrop and setting for my childhood and teenage years. Unfortunately, in the late 1960s, our store was also the setting for considerable heartbreak and even tragedy. But for the decade and a half up until then, it was quite simply the most wonderful place in the world.

****

HARD WORKING, endearing.

That pretty much describes my parents, Harry and Midge Braverman.

Let's begin with my mother. Unfortunately, I do not have very much information about my mother or her family background. I know that my mother's family, which was Jewish, emigrated from Latvia, in then-imperial Russia, around the turn of the century and settled in Chicago, as did many Russian-Jewish immigrants in the first great wave of Russian-Jewish immigration. I know that she had one sister and one brother. I know that her mother died when she was a teenager in the 1930s, and that she experienced severe emotional difficulties, including a brief hospitalization, because of that traumatic event (although I didn't learn about that until much later).

Nevertheless, she seems to have emerged from those early problems with her upbeat personality intact. I also know that she was extremely bright. Midge's thumbnail biography in her yearbook from the class of 1932 of Marshall High School—which is also about the only reliable source of information I have about her early years—sort of says it all:

"An all-around girl? That's Midge. Her radiant personality, vivid charm, and abounding cheerfulness..."

Evidently, she also had real leadership qualities; witness the fact that her classmates elected her senior class vice president. For the record, Midge was also secretary of the student council, president of the Girl Reserves, and vice president of the "M" club, (whatever those were). She also played tennis—well enough to become the women's junior champion of Chicago. Or so I have been told.

4

Apparently, my mother's first ambition was to teach gym, although she seems to have had literary dreams as well:

"…When Midge tires of teaching gym, she will become a journalist."

Unfortunately, like so many women of her generation, and despite being named salutatorian of her class, my mother was never able to actualize any of those early abilities or ambitions after graduating from Marshall in 1932.

I have very little information about what Midge did after graduating from high school, other than that I know that she was accepted into the University of Chicago—a notable achievement in and of itself—and entered, but did not complete her studies. I do know that she moved to Los Angeles at the beginning of World War II and took a job with one of the military auxiliary services in 1943, which is how she met my father.

Clearly my mother's early life was not an easy one. I can only imagine how frustrated she was that she was not able to complete her university studies. However, all the difficulties and frustrations she experienced before I knew her—or at least knew her well—did not seem to have affected her effervescent demeanor.

"…Radiant personality…vivid charm…abounding cheerfulness…"

Or, as my brother Roger put it simply, "Devoted, cheerful, caring…That was Mom."

That pretty well describes the smiling, animated woman that the customers of both of my parents' candy stores saw, and the one that kept them coming back for the better part of two decades.

That's also pretty much the woman I knew and saw when I was growing up in the 1950s in my parents' first house, right behind their first store on 164th Street and 84th Avenue, in a pleasant, middle-class Queens neighborhood known as Jamaica, just south of Grand Central Parkway (yes, it is adjacent to Jamaica Estates, the area in which the current occupant of The White House was raised). What they didn't see, and I only saw later, after the failure of our second store in Flushing, was that there was a small, hairline crack behind my mother's radiant smile, and one that would ultimately split wide open.

Growing up in Jamaica, I had, of course, heard vague references to the aforementioned psychological problems. Also, in 1959, when I was eight, my mother went away on a mysterious "vacation" for several months. What I didn't know, and what my father and brother kept from me, was that she was undergoing treatment for a nervous breakdown.

Certainly I knew that *something* was wrong with Midge—and so obviously did my father, although, unsurprisingly, he did not mention it. This was still the pre-*Dr. Phil* days. However, my mother returned to the store soon enough, with her redoubtable smile intact. Life went on. Besides, there was too much to do, both at the store as well as at my neighborhood school, P.S. 131, where I was a steady if not stellar learner; and too much fun was to be had playing stickball and touch football in the schoolyard, or baseball at the nearby field of Jamaica High School under the watchful eye of Joe Austin, the man who became my second father, so to speak, for me to worry about anything very much.

Anyway, how much can an eight-year-old boy know about psychology? As far as I knew, my mother was fine, at least until the early 60s, when I began to wonder how psychologically fit she really was. Moreover, the Yankees were winning, as they always seemed to be in the late 1950s and early 1960s, and despite her seemingly never-ending duties at the store, she somehow found the time—and the money—to take me to Yankee Stadium to watch the Bronx Bombers play in the World Series on four separate occasions while my father stayed behind to tend the store.

****

MY FATHER Harry probably penned the truest words about himself in an adult education course he took at Touro College when he was in his late 60s in an effort to remedy some of the holes in his spotty earlier education.

"Persistence is a good character[istic] to have," he wrote in response to the unknown essay theme, in his somewhat discombobulated but sincere writing style.

"If one is knocked down, one must get up and try again," he declared. "First knowing you are right and keeping on trying (sic)," he continued, in an upbeat mode, "is a quality that will give you reward (sic) in the end."

As I saw at first hand for the first fifteen years of my life, persistence was certainly a quality my father had in spades. He also most certainly got knocked down—twice—as I also saw all too closely when the first, then the second of his candy stores failed.

Whether my father received his just reward in life is debatable, particularly in the light of those unfortunate and traumatic events—as well as the additional challenges he experienced on account of my mother's delicate disposition and various hospitalizations.

Still, it is a measure of his inner resilience and redoubtable optimism—two of his other great qualities—that he wrote the above words after those business knockdowns, as well as my mother's final traumatic breakdown.

Yes, persistent my father was, and resilient, too. Indeed if I learned anything from working side by side with him in both of his stores, it was the importance of persistence, hard work, and, in the words of the immortal Bobby Jones, the great golfer, to play the ball where it lies.

When I think of my father, the phrase unsung hero comes to mind. For as long as I knew him, he was never the center of attention. He would rarely complain, and I cannot recall a single time when he asked for anything material for himself. In fact, the most demanding I ever heard him get was when he asked my mother to stop talking so he could listen to the television.

My father did not have much opportunity for academic learning. However, he was adept at extracting life's lessons from the events which marked his personal journey. My father's core values were loyalty, unselfishness, persistence, and hard work. Where another man might have quit, he stood by my mother through all of our trials and tribulations, including her great breakdown in 1968. If I know little about my mother's early years, I know even less about my father's. Not only did he talk less about himself than Midge, he talked less, period. It's not that he was reluctant to converse, but he would seldom initiate social discourse. Much of what I do know comes from either the notebook of his writings he kept for his senior citizen's course, or from one of my mother's stream-of-consciousness type monologues—when she made any sense.

I do know that Harry was born in Montreal in 1910, the youngest of a family that also included two daughters and two other sons. Like hundreds of thousands of other Russian Jews—including the family of his future wife—his parents, Jacob and Rachel, likely left Russia as a result of the pogroms that swept the tsarist dominions at the end of the nineteenth century—except that instead of going to the United States, they decided to go to Canada. I have one old studio photograph of the seven Bravermans, taken around 1913 or 1914 that shows my Dad at age three or four wearing knickers, along with the rest of the family, including his rather severe-looking father and mother, and his sister and two brothers, in the manner of the time.

The Bravermans look fairly content there. However, they couldn't have been too happy because not long after that photo was shot my grandfather decided to pick up sticks and move to Brooklyn, where young Harry grew up and went to school. Following his graduation from high school in 1928, Harry, who apparently had artistic ambitions, attended the Pratt Institute in Brooklyn. Unfortunately, however, he had to drop out. He held a series of jobs after that, including one at a nearby candy store where he got his introduction to his future trade.

Harry enlisted in the Army in 1942, after the U.S. entered World War II. However, perhaps because of his age—he was already in his early 30s—he did not deploy overseas, but was instead sent to an Army Air Force base near Lake Mojave in the California desert, where he served in the Quartermaster Corps. Although not one to talk much about his Army life, I do recall him complaining about the strict discipline, as well as the hardship of working in the intense heat of the Western desert. However, he seems to have done reasonably well, rising to the rank of corporal, before being discharged at the end of the war in 1945.

Possibly my father's service in the Quartermaster Corps also whetted his desire to open a candy store of his own in New York. After a few years of fairly low-end jobs and a lot of scrimping and saving he did just that in 1950, opening our first store in the then up-and-coming middle class neighborhood of Jamaica, and moving to a two bedroom apartment just behind the business, with his and Midge's first child, my brother, Roger.

The store, which was known as Harry and Midge's, was a modest success, and three years later, in 1953, two years after I was born, my father was able to purchase his own attached house a half mile away. The Bravermans had bought their own slice of the American Dream.

Or so they thought.

****

IF THERE is a more difficult way of supporting a family of four than owning and operating one's own candy store, I am not aware of it. Harry and Midge's was very much a full-time operation. From 6 a.m. to 10 p.m., six and a half days a week (closing at 2 p.m. on Sunday), week after week, for the better part of two decades, my father toiled behind the counter of his candy store to put food on the table, clothing on our backs, and a roof over our heads, all the while dealing with the insane economics of making a go of his quirky enterprise.

How he managed to do this was an ongoing source of amazement to me. I had difficulty fathoming how my father could earn enough money to stay afloat, as well as pay the mortgage when the profit margin on most of his merchandise could generally be measured in pennies. Nevertheless, somehow he managed to do it.

One of the reasons, if not the main reason, was that Harry and Midge's was based on teamwork, being run by one parent and one son at scheduled intervals each day. We four Bravermans were all in it together. This was never more apparent than on Sundays, when all of us would get up before dawn and marshal our collective forces for the herculean task of assembling the Sunday newspapers, as my brother Roger tellingly relates:

"Our day started at 5 a.m. every Sunday. The routine was always the same. Rise and shine, pick up the bundles, set up each section on the soda stools, and fold them together to make the complete Sunday *New York Mirror,* Sunday *New York Herald Tribune,* and the real behemoth of the group, the five hundred page plus Sunday *New York Times.*

"We needed to finish by a certain time—6 a.m.," Roger remembers. "And we did. You see, my father had his own system. He wrote down the names of the people because they ordered them in advance. And it worked."

No, those mornings weren't much "fun." But they were satisfying in their own way. When we finally closed the store around 2 p.m., we genuinely felt we had accomplished something. Occasionally—very occasionally—there was time for collective R&R. During the summer months, we would drive to Jones Beach and spend the day there, recuperating. That was nice.

****

To be sure, seeing the family at work and being an active part of that process helped to inculcate me with my parents' intense work ethic, an ethic I like to think I have brought forward into adulthood. By the time I was ten, I was a candy store pro. There was no aspect of the business I could not handle. Sometimes, depending on the day's traffic and my father's whims, I would work the front of the store, helping to sell merchandise and operate the cash register, or I would work the soda fountain, pulling sodas and making egg creams, which I especially delighted in doing, while acquiring something of a reputation for my fountain prowess.

Other times Dad would send me to the back storeroom, where I would assemble the weekly magazine return, carefully recording the weekly sales of each of the myriad magazines we stocked for our publications supplier, Hamilton News. I suppose you could call it child labor—I started working in the store in 1959 when I was eight--but I didn't mind because I knew I was making a contribution to my family's welfare and upkeep.

In the meantime, I had also inadvertently received the dubious benefit of something like an Advanced Placement class in sex education, thanks to the piles of pornographic material which my father deemed too risqué to stock in the front and which I occasionally found myself rifling through out of morbid curiosity. (Needless to say, my father was none the wiser.)

Somewhere in there I even managed to get a real education at my local elementary school, Public School 131. One of the city's better elementary schools, 131 was housed in an imposing Collegiate Gothic building ten blocks and a quick walk away. Every day after class during the school year I would run home and do my schoolwork—perhaps after stopping in the school's expansive asphalt schoolyard for a quick game of stickball with one of my discounted Pensy Pinkies, before sidling off to the store for my daily shift.

Over the weekend and during the summer, I had more time to play stickball or baseball, as well as to watch my favorite team, the Yankees, who were then pretty much clobbering everyone in sight. So it wasn't as if I was tethered to the store. Nevertheless, come every Sunday morning, at 4:30 a.m., there I would be, helping my parents and Roger stack those heaving mounds of *New York Times* and *Daily News* papers.

****

SPEAKING of my family, I should say something about my brother at this point. It has been said that if your sibling is more than five years older or younger than you, it is difficult to form a close bond with him or her, and I suppose with the seven years difference between us that was true of my older brother Roger and me. We were not close, but we were close enough, and we spent enough time together for me to admire him and for him to be a powerful role model for me, particularly in the athletic sphere, at least until he went off to college in 1962.

My brother, it so happens, was athletically gifted. He was ambidextrous and a legitimate switch hitter in baseball. Though, like me, he only stood five foot six, he was incredibly strong. As a runner, he also had lightning speed. And he had surprising power from the right side of the plate for someone of his stature. From the left side, he hit for a better average.

He was also an excellent role model as a group leader. At the baseball field—when he had time to play—he would leave his team and play with me and my friends. He was great. I just wished that he was younger. There are only so many ways in which a seventeen-year-old can relate to a ten-year-old, but he tried. I am sure he also would have been happier if he had a brother who was closer to him in age as well.

****

INEVITABLY my classmates, particularly those with sweet teeth—in other words, just about everyone—would envy my proximity to all that ice cream, chocolate bars, and the like, and the hefty amounts of these my jealous classmates presumed I was wolfing down every day at the family store.

Hence my friends' surprise when I informed them that I rarely if ever sampled the wares, not because I didn't want to—believe me I did—but because I didn't wish to sink our modest enterprise by consuming the tiny profit margin with those delectable items (although I confess that I acquired a hankering for ice cream that has remained with me until this day). As a small boy there might be no meaningful way for me to increase business, but I would be damned if I was going to consume what little we were able to clear.

Unquestionably, my proudest contribution to our family business was my egg creams. This formerly popular drink—— virtually unknown outside of New York City—is comprised of a delicious concoction of seltzer, milk, and usually chocolate syrup. The difference between a mediocre egg cream and a great tasting one is the amount of milk used. I tended to use a little more milk than most of our many competitors, which cut down our profit margin somewhat, but the trade-off was the steady flow of customers who came into the store asking for one of "Jesse's specials."

I guess I may not have had the easiest life of my classmates at P.S. 131—as far as I knew I was the only one who had a steady part-time job--but I couldn't really complain. In their own way, my parents had achieved the American Dream, or at least a modest version of it, and generally I was happy to help out.

****

UNFORTUNATELY, we Bravermans were about to receive two very hard back-to-back lessons in the *other* side of the American Dream, and the evolving character of the American enterprise—including our bellwether business, newspaper sales.

The first lesson came in the form of two large, competing chain stores, a Woolworth's and an A&P supermarket, which arrived in our neighborhood in rapid succession in 1961, the same year I turned ten, and which immediately began vacuuming up our sizable cigarette business—this was still the era when one half of American adults smoked--by underselling us.

Almost overnight, it seemed, our cigarette business was gone. I didn't understand. One night my father laid it out for me. He explained that our two new unwelcome commercial neighbors were selling cigarettes as "loss leaders," meaning that they were deliberately selling cigarettes at a loss in order to induce the tobacco-addicted customers to purchase other items.

And so, as we could sadly see, the customers were. People, it seemed, were more interested in convenience than loyalty. Instead of going round to the various Mom and Pop stores— including *our* Mom and Pop store—to collect what they or their kids needed in the course of a leisurely Saturday afternoon, now they could get everything they needed at once at Woolworth's and A&P, loyalty be damned. It wasn't fair.

Suddenly the customers who used to come for cigarettes and newspapers and maybe a Pensy-Pinkie for Little Bobbie or a doll for Little Sue—and maybe one of my patented milk-laden egg creams while they were at it—only came by for the papers, and that's it. As was her wont, my mother kept up her brave smile while my father stoically continued with his chores. However, very soon even I could see that we were in trouble. Our old faithful National Cash Register just wasn't ringing up as many sales as it used to.

And then one day in the fall of 1961, it stopped ringing altogether, we were out of business, and my father pulled down the steel shutters over Harry and Midge's one last time.

****

HOWEVER, the American Dream wasn't entirely over for the Bravermans, just as yet, thanks to the help of my mother's sister, my Aunt Mae, and her husband, Ben Polikoff. My Uncle Ben could have been the model for the character who told Dustin Hoffman in "The Graduate" that his future lay in plastics, except that *that* Ben, my Uncle Ben, actually made it happen. Plastics had made him a multi-millionaire. Although I am sure that my mother wasn't crazy about the idea, Ben kindly offered to lend Harry and Midge the money for a down payment on our second candy store, and they accepted.

And so, one joyous day in the fall of 1962, my father pried open the shutters of our new location on 46th Avenue in Flushing, about five miles away from the first store, and the Bravermans were back in the candy store business. As it happened, the Yankees were world champions again that year, and as far as I was concerned we had won the World Series along with them. Harry and Midge's Candy Store had received a second lease on life.

In no time at all, our family was back up to speed, and the neighborhood kids were filing in to buy their Jujyfruits and Pensy-Pinkies while their parents stopped by to buy their newspapers and cigarettes. Once again, all was well with the world. While my father, my brother, and I supplied the elbow grease behind the new operation, my mother provided the ready smile and personal touch for which she was known, along with some new creative and effective marketing ideas.

One of these was a model building contest aimed at the store's sizable, model-minded contingent, judged by Midge, which quickly drew dozens of eager entrants. All entrants were immediately rewarded by having their work displayed in the store window; in a smart and ecumenical touch, entrants did not have to purchase their model building kits at our store. After several weeks my mother would take a hard look at all of those entries, which numbered up to several dozen, and declare the two or three "winners."

Midge would then call the lucky kids to come down to the store to collect their prize: a free milkshake or ice cream soda. And if the winners wished to bring their parents along, so much the better. Their work would then be placed in the window for an indefinite period, so they could bring their admiring (and envious) friends around to further show off their masterpieces, and maybe grab an egg cream afterward.

Clearly, my mother had a flair for the candy store business. Another proof of this was her clever method for dealing with the age old "browsing" conundrum. Like other candy stores, Harry and Midge's had a large number of customers who were fond of perusing the magazines on offer without any intention of buying them. That was all right as long as there was only one kid flipping through *Mad* or *Model Building Monthly* or whatever, but if there were more browsers it would, understandably, tend to get on my parents' nerves.

However, whereas another, less child-friendly owner might respond by loudly reprimanding or shooing the non-paying readers away, my mother would simply walk over while the rest of us looked on with knowing smiles and ask one of the eager readers in a voice just loud enough for the others to hear, "May I see your library card?" That usually did the trick.

And so, with Harry's steady hand once again on the wheel, Midge's customer relations skills, and the hard work of all of us, by the end of 1962, the second incarnation of Harry and Midge's soon got up to cruising speed. In fact, the Flushing store did even better than its predecessor, at least at first. Slowly but surely the shop also began to pay for itself.

****

NOW that I was slightly older—I was still all of eleven--I worked even more hours than I had in Jamaica, putting in up to four or five hours a day. This was in part to make up for the absence of my brother, Roger, who went off to college that fall. For my efforts, I was given a $10 a week allowance, a considerable sum in that day and age. I didn't mind: I was needed. Simple as that.

What about school? Fair question. In all honesty, I have to admit, I was not the best student. I like to think that I was as bright as my more assiduous classmates (such as my coauthor and fellow P.S. 131 classmate), but for one reason or another, my grades were generally in the "Good" or "Fair" category. My mind was simply on other things.

I did well enough to gain admission to the three-year Special Progress program, an enhanced curriculum at my next school, Van Wyck Junior High School, on the other side of Jamaica. Given a choice I chose the so-called Three Year S.P. program over the Two Year accelerated track which allowed one to skip a grade. Although the notion of skipping a grade was attractive, I was concerned that doing that would force me to compete with older ball players, if and when I played Varsity: remember, baseball was everything for me. As I look back, while I do not regret passing on accelerating my junior high experience, I do wish I had worked harder in school.

In a way my real school was the candy store.

In the meantime, the store continued to do well. Occasionally my parents allowed me to "freelance" for other friends' families' businesses, as I did with hilarious results when I helped the parents of my friend Jimmy Gonedes with their lucrative street-cart food business on Columbus Day of 1964. Working for the

Gonedeses, a savvy second generation Greek-American family who had carved out their own slice of the American Dream, was a veritable army of street peddlers of varying ages—and, as I was to learn, ethics—who, after setting up shop at their assigned locations, including many prime Manhattan street corners, spent the day dispensing ice cream, hot dogs, soda, juice, pretzels, chestnuts, and the like, and making a tidy profit for themselves— as well as for the Gonedeses.

That day, Columbus Day 1964, I became another one of the Gonedeses' foot soldiers. Having heard of the possible windfall to be gained from manning one of the Gonedeses' mobile food carts, I reported for vending duty at dawn at the food cart assembly point along the parade route on upper Fifth Avenue, where I proudly took charge of my aromatic cart from the beaming Jimmy Gonedes himself.

After receiving my battle orders from Jimmy—which essentially entailed selling as much as I could as fast as I could—I enthusiastically wheeled my five-hundred-pound plus food cart to my assigned spot several blocks past the crowds of onlookers who comprised my future clientele, feeling very much like a mid-nineteenth century California prospector.

Or rather, I *began* to wheel the cart into place. What I hadn't counted on—and what my friend had failed to tell me—was that particular stretch of Fifth Avenue was made from cobblestone, not asphalt, and that one had to pull the bulging, top-heavy cart very slowly over the uneven surface lest it begin to rock and topple over, spilling its contents onto the street, and taking the hapless operator along with it.

Which of course is exactly what happened next. Once that cart started rocking there was nothing I could do to right it; my diminutive body mass made the spectacular climax all the more inevitable. One moment there I was, waving to my potential customers, as I pulled the cart with one arm, visions of instant wealth dancing in my head; the next, I was tearfully collecting my spilled wares, while those same, now lost customers looked on with pity.

Worst of all, I thought to myself, as I gathered the soiled—and presumably spoiled—pretzels and the like, what would I tell Jimmy and his family? Here they had taken a chance on me and I had let them down while losing a sizable amount of merchandise. Woe was me.

Sure enough, after a few minutes, Jimmy, who had seen the accident from his vantage point up the avenue, came rushing up to the scene of the culinary contretemps. However, instead of administering a tongue lashing, as his tearful associate expected, the canny Greek took a quick look around, righted the cart, and began collecting the salvageable merchandise, including the myriad pretzels scattered around the street, and cleaning—or should one say, *wiping*—them as best he could.

"What are we going to do with those pretzels?" I asked, as Jimmy wiped one of the dirtied pretzels against his leg.

"Sell'em," he answered, without missing a beat.

And so I did, albeit with considerable qualms, once we had wheeled the cart to a "safe" new location down the avenue from my original spot.

As luck or the furies had it, the first customer for one of my tidied-up pretzels was a beneficently smiling and hungry Catholic nun. Had I mortgaged my chance of an afterlife for a few lousy bucks, I wondered, as the sister ambled off, contentedly munching away on the dubious edible.

I guess I still have to find that out.

****

However, for sheer hilarity, or absurdity, none of my adolescent adventures rivaled that of my improbable collaboration with my friend Jimmy on a project for the 1965 Van Wyck Junior High School Science Fair. As at many, if not most, other American schools during the early-to-mid-60s, when the Space Race with the Soviets was on, Science was the holy grail at Van Wyck. Consequently, all students were encouraged, if not required, to create—or perhaps conjure up is a better way to put it—a project for the vaunted fair.

18

Not being especially science-minded, Jimmy and I, who had decided to submit a joint project on the supposition that two empty brains were better than one, were stumped, until my ever-helpful mother came along with a bright idea. She suggested that we consider an ant farm for our entry. Why not?

Upon further inquiry we learned that one could actually send away for an ant farm. And so we did. Sure enough, the ant farm arrived, complete with hundreds of bona fide ants. Unfortunately we hadn't figured out the next step: as I said, science was not our forte. The ants would have to fend for themselves until we decided what we wanted to do with them.

Finally, with about ten days to go until our mutual entomological debut, Jimmy and I started talking about some of the experiments we could possibly perform with our idling society of arthropods. The next day, I went to Jimmy's house in order to continue our deliberations. However instead of his usual confident self, he was pale and flustered. Obviously something untoward had taken place.

It had. "Steven," he confessed, referring to his youngest brother, "flushed the ant farm down the toilet." Of course I thought that Jimmy, a big kidder, was kidding. "Yeah right," I replied. Then Jimmy pulled out the soggy remains of our projected science fair entry. Poor ants. Poor us. We decided to place an immediate long-distance phone call to secure a replacement ant colony.

Each day, we checked for the delivery to no avail. Then, thankfully, two days before the day of judgment, the new ant colony arrived at Jimmy's house. Suddenly possessed with a desire to give his new guests a proper home, Jimmy immediately dived into one of his family's closets, extracted a hanger, bent it, and began carving away. Soon, he had constructed a labyrinth of subterranean passageways for our new friends which would have made any Queen Ant proud.

Then we really went to work. Employing a toy maze I got from the candy store, we collaborated on a realistic-sounding, if utterly nonsensical essay that described how a typical ant tenant could locate food in the maze, and another for how he could socialize with his fellow ants. It was great.

Finally the day when we had to explain the project to our seventh grade science class arrived. I had to admit the finished product was impressive. I let Jimmy do most of the talking, lest I start giggling. I have to admit, Jimmy did a very good job. Indeed, he did such a good job that several days later we received the incredible news that we had been selected as one of the two science-minded teams who would be representing Van Wyck in the borough-wide science fair.

Our fame, as such, proved to be short-lived. Although we were confident enough when we arrived for the borough competition, it was immediately clear that we were out of our league. The kid next to us had some sort of nuclear device demonstrating the peaceful uses of this harnessed natural powerhouse. "What the hell am I doing here?" I wondered out loud.

My preternaturally confident friend, however, would not be deterred. When, after we finally stepped up to explain our contribution to modern science, one of the four teacher-judges asked us about our subject insect's ability to hear, Jimmy launched into a lengthy, impassioned, and totally nonsensical disquisition about insect antennae and sound waves, while I stood mutely by.

To make a long story short, we didn't win. Nevertheless I got an A in Science. That had never happened before. Thank you Jimmy. Thank you ants. (What happened to the ants? Don't ask.)

****

ALAS, as it turned out, my days of making egg creams were not long to be, and neither was the second incarnation of my parents' candy store. Once again, just as had occurred with the Jamaica store, supermarkets and discount stores encroached on our business. Once again, we were losing money, Jesse's famous egg creams notwithstanding.

Another event that hurt us was the month-long New York City newspaper strike in September of 1965. When the dust had cleared, six newspapers, including the iconic *Herald Tribune*, the *World Telegram, The Long Island Star Journal,* and *The New York Mirror* had folded, so to speak.

Gone, too, was a sizable chunk of our store's business. Gone were the days when customers bought two newspapers. Now, in addition to doing without a second paper, some customers also did without that extra pack of cigarettes. Our business was shrinking and there was simply nothing we could do to stop it. Seeing this gave me an awful sense of *déjà vu*. After all, I had seen this happen several years before. Now that I was fourteen, the process impacted me all the more.

My mother kept her brave smile while my father kept stoically plugging away. However, as I could immediately see when I turned the corner on 46th Avenue and opened the door with a brave smile the afternoon after school to take up my shift on our sinking ship, we had taken a torpedo beneath the water line. It was only a matter of time before we sank. The place which had been the center of my universe ever since I could remember—my parents' beloved candy store, and all its quirks—was dying, and so was our claim on the American Dream.

Such was life, as I was beginning to understand. Maybe life *wasn't* fair.

It turned out that rumors of the demise of Harry and Midge's second candy store were premature. Although our neighborhood fountain never quite recovered from the '65 strike, it lingered on for another four years before shuttering in 1969, the year I went off to college.

But we certainly had a good run.

And for the record I still make a mean egg cream.

CHAPTER 2:
A COACH NAMED JOE

Let me paint the scene. South Jamaica, fifty or sixty years ago. Middle class. Poor. Immigrants. The principal influence was the family and the church or the synagogue. No one had an automobile or a TV. In that environment picture a guy who was born in Queens. He had been a semi-professional [baseball] player. He lives with his sisters in an old house. In time he [gets a job as a manager] at the Piels Brewery. And he spends his time putting together baseball teams. Listen to the names: the Dwarves, the Elves, the Shamrocks, the Erins, the Blarney Stones. Even the girls had a team…

> —the late Mario Cuomo, Governor of New York, and one of Joe's kids, speaking to *The New York Times* on the occasion of the dedication of a Queens, New York park to his childhood coach and mentor, Joe Austin (1984)

OK. You've got a good picture of the main center of my universe when I was growing up: Harry and Midge's Candy Store and the devoted couple who ran it, my parents, Harry and Midge Braverman. Now it's time to turn the retrospective spotlight to the center of my parallel universe, the baseball field, and the towering figure who tended it and served as my other principal adult role model, Joe Austin.

To get a good picture of *that* world and the seemingly ageless man at the center of it, we need to turn the camera back a bit, to the late 1940s, before either I or Harry and Midge's were born. Same neighborhood. Just a little further back. Great. Now let's zoom in…

OK. If you had happened to walk by the baseball field behind the towering collegiate Gothic main building of Jamaica High School, located on 164ᵗʰ Place near Grand Central Parkway, in Jamaica, Queens, on a Saturday morning in July or August, 1949, around, say, eight o'clock, you would have likely seen a man of medium height with prematurely white hair, dressed in a T-shirt and khaki pants, determinedly raking the pitcher's mound, tending to the chalk lines, or otherwise getting the field into playing shape.

And if it had rained the night before, as it sometimes does in New York at that time of year, and the field was covered in puddles, he might have been draining some of those.

Additionally, you might have noticed that the man was wearing steel-tipped shoes.

You also might have noticed that that the man was very focused on what he was doing, almost as if he were tending his own garden.

And if you had waited a little longer, until say nine a.m., you probably would have seen a group of youngsters ranging in age from twelve to eighteen gather around the same man while eagerly pounding their gloves. And they would have been wearing uniforms with resoundingly Irish names like the Dwarves and the Elves and the Shamrocks, even if some of them didn't look particularly Irish.

Hmmm. Doesn't that kid look Jewish? And isn't that one a girl?

And then, if you had waited a little longer, you would have seen a couple of the kids—there might have been ten or fifteen by then—engage in a little exercise in which the two kids would stand about twenty feet away from the man and throw the ball at him, and he would hit grounders to these "infielders."

And two other kids standing behind those kids would retrieve the balls that the "infielders" missed. "Pepper," it used to be called back in the day.

And then if you waited a little longer—there would be even more kids by now, maybe twenty or thirty—you would see all of them (or most of them) arrayed around the outfield, waiting for the man with prematurely white hair to hit fly balls or line drives to them, which he proceeded to do with preternatural accuracy.

Just before the man would hit the ball, he would signal to the player he was targeting whether he was going to hit it to the left or to the right. That would be the boy or girl's cue to start running in that direction as fast as he or she could. And they would start running. And somehow the man timed each ball so that each one would descend exactly at the spot where he wanted.

"He always hit them in places that were challenging," as one of Joe's kids recalled years later, still in awe of the man's skill. "They were never hit so far away that they were impossible to catch; neither were they hit so easily that I could catch them at a trot. He never missed the ball or even hit grounders."

Of course you wouldn't know it unless you could see into the future, but one of those teenagers dashing around, shagging balls would be a future governor of New York by the name of Mario Cuomo.

****

GOT the picture? Good. Now, let's pull the retrospective camera back and move forward fifteen years or so to, say 1965, and zoom in, and what would you see? Same man, except that now his hair is a little whiter. And yes, he would still be surrounded by kids… And the kids would still be as eager. And the line drives just as accurate.

And one of those boys, of course, would be me, Jesse Braverman.

And the man with the prematurely white hair? That would be the late Joseph Austin, better known to the thousands of kids he coached over six decades simply as Joe.

AS is often the case with legends, the file of known biographical facts about Joe Austin is somewhat slim. What I know is as follows:

24

I know that Austin was born in 1904 in South Jamaica, Queens. We know that he attended Jamaica High School, when that once great high school—which I attended myself between 1966 and 1969 and where I played on the varsity baseball team—was located on Hillside Avenue before it moved to its present campus. One of ten children, Joe was forced to drop out of J.H.S. after the tenth grade, a common enough occurrence in the 1920s.

"I had to drop out of Jamaica High School after my first year," Austin recalled, matter-of-factly, in a rare formal interview he gave many years later. That was the end of his formal schooling. "But in those days, high school was a luxury. You had to get a job to help out at home with the bills."

I don't know how active Joe was in school sports; presumably he was too busy helping to support his large family to spend much time in the school yard. However, like so many young Americans of the 1920s, he picked up the sports bug, particularly the bug for baseball. And he became an avid fan of The New York Giants. Years later, Austin would speak in reverential terms to us about the Giants' long-reigning manager, John McGraw, who helmed the team for a record thirty years. Joe also seemed to have picked up a ken for playing himself.

In the meantime, Joe helped support his family by moving through a series of skilled and semi-skilled jobs. One of those early jobs, probably the best of the lot, was as a worker with the old Boyce Motor Meter Company, the long defunct manufacturing company that used to turn out those old, lollipop-looking "MotoMeters," or temperature meters, back in the Jazz Age. Perhaps the most attractive aspect of that job for Joe was that Boyce had a baseball team. He joined it.

Joe was able to further pursue his passion for baseball by playing on a number of semi-professional teams around the tri-state region. He wasn't The Natural, but he was good. "He was a good solid third baseman," said Mario Cuomo, who probably knew as much about Austin's statistics as anyone else. "He would never hit a home run for you," said Cuomo in an interview with *The New York Times* in 1984, in conjunction with a ceremony for Austin, at which the playground next to the Jamaica High ball field was named in his honor, confirming his status as a local hero. "But [he] always batted .270 or .280," added the former governor, who played several seasons of semi-pro ball himself, before heading off into the political arena.

Who said I would never hit a home run? One imagines that would be the feisty Austin's response to his most famous alumnus's faint praise. Then again, of course, it was not how Austin played the game that mattered the most to Cuomo. It was how he taught it: somewhere around 1930 the scrappy second-generation Irishman also picked up a ken for coaching, the activity that would become his true life's passion. Also, as it turned out, he was pretty good at it.

Then the Great Depression hit and in 1931 Joe was laid off from Boyce. So Joe hit the pavement again, looking for a job. Hard times. That was part of Joe's curriculum vitae too.

Sudsy times too. In 1933 Prohibition ended, enabling the old Piels Brewery—also known to New Yorkers of a certain age as the makers of Piels Real Draft and Draft Ale—in Bushwick, Brooklyn to reopen. Shifting his diurnal clock, Joe took a job shortly thereafter as a dispatcher on the midnight shift, aka "the graveyard shift." Evidently the job suited him, and vice versa, because he never took another, remaining with Piels for over thirty years, until his retirement from the working world in 1967.

Working the graveyard shift presumably made it difficult for Joe to play on the Piels baseball team. But that was OK because it enabled him to realize his other passion—his passion for coaching—on a grand scale, putting together a raft of organized and semi-organized sports teams for the youngsters of his Queens neighborhood, particularly baseball teams. Austin also coached basketball and football, but baseball was his first love, and that is what he concentrated on. At one time, this one-man athletic camp coached as many as seven teams.

Joe never married, choosing to live in the same South Jamaica house where he grew up with two of his sisters. As he was fond of saying, he was "married to the game." He never had any children of his own, except for the literally hundreds of children who would show up every spring and summer for the chance to play with this one-man athletic association.

Whatever funds Austin was able to set aside from his modest salary, he spent on purchasing equipment for his constantly self-replenishing sports progeny.

That, essentially, is all that is known—or at least all that I know—about Joe Austin. In a sense, that is all one needs to know about him. He lived for his kids, and he lived for the game, in that order.

That was it for Austin. For over fifty years, from the time he first started coaching in 1933, to his technical "retirement" from the game in 1984 and beyond—from the Great Depression through the Second World War through the Korean War and the Vietnam War and the beginning of the end of the Cold War—he was there for his kids, teaching them about baseball. And, of course, about life.

"As he got older, he got more tired," said David Heckendorn, who played for Austin in the 60s, and who went on to teach music at Jamaica High School and become a successful jazz musician. "But still, everyday, he would be at the field with his newspaper, his bats, and his balls, surrounded by kids of all ages."

What a comfort, what a sense of security, it was for me and generations of young boys to know that each and every day, we could walk or ride our bikes to the field, and we would find Joe there to welcome us every spring and summer and provide us with a full day of baseball practice and games.

Joe became part of my world, or perhaps I should say I became part of Joe's world in 1956, when I was five and Roger introduced me to him, and I started attending his informal pick-up games. Later, in 1962, I joined Joe's uniformed team, the Emeralds. I continued to play with the Emeralds for another six years, through my junior high and high school years, while also playing with the Jamaica varsity baseball team, the Beavers.

****

27

I HAVE lots of memories of Joe, of course, some of which I will weave into the pages that follow. So let me give the floor, so to speak, to some of Joe's other kids.

Unsurprisingly, many of Joe's progeny have crystal clear memories of *their* first encounter with the man who would become a landmark in their lives.

My old friend Peter Lord, with whom I would both play for Joe and on the Jamaica High varsity team, certainly recalls the day in 1965 when he first tried out for Joe, who was already 62, as if it were yesterday. And boy, does he remember those fungos.

"As I walked onto the field I saw something I had never seen prior or since. It was a sight to behold and almost indescribable," says Peter, who went on to become an accountant. "I saw a mix of batting practice, infielders being hit ground balls, and outfielders shagging fly balls.

"At the center of all this activity was this older man in a baseball cap hitting balls with a fungo[2] bat. *Never* have I seen such precision. Each of his swings launched a baseball like a guided missile. Was I dreaming? Did I just enter baseball heaven?!

"But that was just the beginning," Lord recalls with wonder. "Joe halted the practice and told his players to line up one behind the other in left field. When he signaled, each player started racing toward center field while Joe hit a Mickey Mantle-like fly ball. If you were running at full speed, your glove would meet the ball perfectly in center field. One after the other!

"Then came the infield work out," says Lord. "Joe hitting one ground ball after the next, with the players fielding and throwing in a perfectly synchronized movement. And then came the grand finale: Joe hitting one perfectly placed foul ball after the other for his catcher to run after and catch."

Up until that moment, the awestruck fourteen year old had escaped Austin's notice. Finally, Austin came over, introduced himself, and extended his hand to Lord as the other players and I continued to practice in the background.

---

[2] Fungo: a form of self-hitting baseball which is used primarily to provide fielding practice.

"He sent me to my position at shortstop, gave me an Austin-style workout, [and] sent me to the plate for some hitting," Lord says.

At the end, Austin came over and said to Lord simply, "Welcome to the Emeralds."

Young Peter Lord was in baseball heaven, along with the rest of us cowhide munchkins.

Today there are hundreds of living Austin alumni ranging in age from their forties to their nineties who have similar memories.

****

BASEBALL and his kids. For sixty years, that was it for Joe. He lived for the game, and for his kids.

"I once asked Joe how come he never married," says David Heckendorn. "He said, 'I don't think a woman would have been able to accept the way I wanted to live my life.' That way of giving so unselfishly of his time and resources made each of us feel special."

"There was only one Joe," says Tony Macaluso, an Austin alumnus and retired Nassau County policeman, who, like many if not most of Austin's alumni, speaks about his former coach and mentor with enthusiasm. In particular, Macaluso recalls Joe's ecumenism. "He didn't care what religion, race or sex you were. You were welcome."

Leslie Mills, who played on one of Joe's scrub teams,[3] can testify to that. "I was only twelve years old when I started chasing balls for Joe," she says. "He was the most generous man I ever knew."

Lew Suber, a retired postal worker, and an African-American who, at a time when prejudice against black people was still commonplace, even in New York, found himself welcome on Joe's field, can also testify to Austin's open door policy. "He gave

---

[3] Scrub team: a team with back-up or substitute players.

29

us *everything*," says Suber. "Gloves if we needed them, knowledge, comradeship."

****

TO BE SURE, a lot of the best stories about Joe revolve around gloves.

Here's mine.

One afternoon in 1958, after I had just joined Joe's World (so to speak), I was a batboy for the Shannons, the team Roger played with. We were on the road that day playing a team called the Saxons. "The road," of course, meant elsewhere in Queens. But for a seven-year-old youngster from Jamaica that was a long way.

The opponent's home field, named Drew Memorial, was adjacent to Van Wyck Expressway, on the way to Kennedy [then Idlewild] Airport. Not the best neighborhood, but that's where the game was, so that's where we went.

I loved to play catch with some of the Shannons before the doubleheaders and was looking forward that day to their high-velocity tosses breaking in my new baseball glove. During the game there was no need for my glove, and I placed it behind the bench. It was a good day, with the Shannons sweeping the twin bill.

So it was. Smiles all around, with handshakes and pats as well. I was smiling, too—until I looked behind the bench and found that my precious glove was not where I had left it. Frantically, I searched through all of the large equipment bags the team had brought with them. Nothing: it had been stolen.

This was my first experience with crime, and it hit hard. Tears welled up in my eyes. How could I tell my parents? The glove, an expensive left-handed model, had been a sacrifice for them, as it was. I decided to conceal the news, but had no long range plan.

The following day, just as Austin was about to begin his usual pepper routine, I sat, gloveless and disconsolate, on the bench, still at a loss as to how to replace the precious glove, convinced that I would not be able to play for the foreseeable future.

I need not have worried.

Joe greeted me as usual. Without saying a word, he reached into his duffel bag and presented me with a brand new glove.

That was Joe Austin.

****

AS any of my fellow Austin alumni could tell you, his generosity didn't stop when the game was over. Every few weeks or so he would take a bunch of us to the Polo Grounds to see "his" Giants, as he called them, paying for everything himself. Other times he would take us to Yankee Stadium or the old Madison Square Garden to watch basketball.

Amazingly Joe paid for everything—tickets, refreshments—himself. "He would know the ticket taker, the usher, the cop on the beat," Austin alumnus and New York City fireman Chris Green remembers. "Sometimes he even knew the players and coaches!"

On other days he would take us to spend the day on Coney Island. A good time was had by all—unless you didn't like riding the Cyclone, the world-famous, vertigo-inducing roller coaster ride. Joe would insist.

As it happened, I was one of the latter group, i.e., the kids who didn't care for the Cyclone, but I pretended I did so that I wouldn't let Joe down. It was on those excursions that the trim, well-disciplined sexagenarian came close to letting his hair down. Not that he got drunk or anything of that sort, but he wasn't above cursing out the umpire at the Polo Grounds when he disagreed with a call, or letting out a shout, along with the rest of us, when he joined us on the Cyclone.

That was also part of the Joe Austin experience.

****

BUT the key attraction, the real treat, of course, was being able to play for Joe. To us, his kids, Joe *was* baseball. He personified the game, and in a way had a genius for it. He demonstrated all the fielding skills used at each position, as well as the proper way to throw.

Oftentimes Austin's "give it your all" philosophy of baseball, coupled with some of the special techniques he taught—or, rather, demonstrated—to his kids, allowed us to overcome the odds and defeat more highly vaunted opponents. One particular instance sticks out in my mind.

There was one Emeralds game, in 1967, when I was pitching and we were playing first place Rosedale, who boasted a Murderers' Row lineup, including a flame-throwing pitcher from Christ the King High School by the name of Bob Shortell. I didn't think that we had much of a chance against such a bigger and talented squad.

Joe thought otherwise, offering his standard advice about not worrying about the other team and instead letting them worry about you. We duly nodded and took the field, while our highly favored opponents in the other dugout laughed and smirked.

In the end, however, it was Joe's kids who would have the last laugh that day. Somehow, using the Austin style of bunting and playing hit and run, we managed to scratch out a pair of runs.

I didn't exactly overpower the opposition, but I was throwing consistent strikes. Our airtight Emeralds defense, led by third baseman Peter Lord, defending the hot corner,[4] turned two key double plays, and the other fielders took care of the rest. The scoreboard told the stunning story at the end of the day: Emeralds 2, Rosedale 0.

Once again, the expert baseball training and philosophy that we had learned served us well.

****

AND YET, as effective a baseball technician and teacher as Joe was, the utility of what the old man taught—or, rather, demonstrated—went far beyond the field.

---

[4] The hot corner: an expression for third base.

"What I got from Joe was the strength of commitment," says David Heckendorn "He imparted a dignity about playing life's game for all it was worth. A game where losing was OK as long as you gave it your best."

"He never yelled at us for making physical mistakes," remembers my friend Bill Rappaport, who played with Joe. What he demanded was 100% effort."

And when he *didn't* get 100%? *That's* when he got upset. Everyone who showed up played—but you better give it your all. That was the core of Joe's philosophy, which he demonstrated by his own (there is no other word) fanatic devotion to the game. Or as he was wont to put it somewhat indelicately: *If you want to play ball, play ball. If you don't want to play ball get the hell off the field.*

In Joe's book, winning was *not* everything, but you'd better give it your all, and no futzing around while you're at it. One Emerald pitcher, one of Joe's stars, discovered this codicil to his regret one day back in 1965, when he reacted to an error by his shortstop by throwing his glove in disgust, Rappaport recalls. "Joe walked up to the mound and told him to 'get the hell off the field.'" To Austin's mind, the pitcher, by dint of his childish behavior, wasn't serious about the game. So out he went. That was Joe too.

Of course, no one could doubt Joe's own commitment to the game, as anyone who saw him during his sixty-some odd seasons of coaching baseball, year after year, beginning with his daily pre-game ablutions, knew. "Every day he would come straight from work," marvels 60s Austin alumnus Michael Schwab, who went on to become a Superior Court judge in Washington State. "You'd come in the morning and see him in the outfield with a sickle, swinging it back and forth, mowing down the weeds. Every day."

Of course, sometimes he did tend to overdo it. "He missed my sister's wedding because he had a doubleheader," his nephew, Garrett, recalls, shaking his head. "And Joe was her godfather!"

Commitment. Tolerance. Selflessness. These are some of the things that Joe's kids learned from him.

****

MIND, the same Austin alumni are agreed, he was no saint. "Joe was not a goody-goody," my friend and fellow Austin alumnus Bruce Lerro declares. "He occasionally cursed, and he did tend to get upset if you did not come on a regular basis." Then, of course, there were the Eddie Stanky-like[5] temper tantrums.

Also, despite their fondness of him, some parents tended to look askance at Joe's offbeat choice of after-hours meeting places, especially Bradley's café. "I was preparing for my Bar Mitzvah when I was twelve," Superior Court Judge Michael Schwab says. "I came home and told my parents how I had just learned to read *Racing Form* at Bradley's Café with my teammates from St. Monica's. They said, "This is our bar mitzvah boy?""

Somehow, with Joe, it evened out.

No, in case you're wondering, Joe didn't produce any major leaguers. "I've produced a lot of cops and firefighters and businessmen," Austin would reply when asked about his placement record. "They're all major leaguers in my book."

And, of course, he did produce one governor. Needless to say, the man who the late Cuomo calls the most important man in his life after his father was in the front row when his former star player was inaugurated in 1981, along with a number of other Austin alumni. "I looked out and saw him rap his left hand into his right palm, the old signal to hit away," said Cuomo. "I stopped and returned the signal and when I did, I saw all the other guys giving the signal. Nobody knew what was going on."

"I was lucky to have known Joe Austin," declares David Heckendorn. "He gave me something that I cannot exactly put into words but I know that has given me a strength and an integrity that has helped me in my life. And if there's a heaven— and I know, Joe, a devout Catholic, believed there was—he's up

---

[5] Eddie Stanky was the pugnacious manager of the Chicago White Sox from 1966 to 1968.

there hitting fungos with a nailed-together wooden bat, or playing 'pepper' in the dusty dirt of an inner-city ball field."

"Joe never had any kids of his own," says Michael Schwab. "But you know about large Irish families? We're *all* his kids."

And I'm one of them. Today his resoundingly humane, redoubtable spirit continues to infuse both my coaching and teaching careers.

CHAPTER 3:
THE BREAKDOWN

CREEDMOOR. Any kid growing up in Queens in the 1960s knew the word. Creedmoor meant crazy, insane. Kids used to joke about it, as in "That guy belongs in Creedmoor." Or, "Man, you belong in Creedmoor."

Creedmoor, of course, refers to the one-hundred-year-old psychiatric hospital located in Queens Village, whose main structure now, as then, consists of a forbidding, twenty-floor, 1930s-era structure overlooking—really overshadowing is a better word—Grand Central Parkway. Anyone driving east or west can see it for miles. The closer you get to it, the scarier it looks.

Today the hospital, officially known as the Creedmoor Psychiatric Center, whose mission, according to its website, is "to provide compassionate, high quality mental health services," has a more benign reputation than it did back then, the result of both the advances in psychiatric medicine that have taken place over the past forty years and the gradual fading of the stigma attached to being mentally ill, as our society itself has, slowly but surely, become compassionate and inclusive itself.

However, there was nothing compassionate about the institution's reputation in the 1950s and 1960s. Creedmoor, which actually was founded by the Lunacy Commission of New York back in 1912—which tells you all you need to know about how American society regarded the mentally ill for the better part of the twentieth century—was simply shorthand for "loony bin," or "a place you don't want to go to," and everything about its physical aspect reinforced that.

Especially those bars…those thick, steel bars running across the width and length of each of Creedmoor's hundreds of windows. That's the thing that really strikes you when you drive past. Hopefully, the quality of the care offered on the other side of those bars is somewhat more compassionate and enlightened than it was back in the 1960s.

I hope at least that Creedmoor officials don't mix patients up and/or misdiagnose them, as befell someone close to me who was incarcerated there at that time. In any case, those horrid bars are still there. I suppose because they have to be.

That was certainly the thing that hit me when I used to pass Creedmoor when the family was heading out to Jones Beach, on one of our all-too-rare family outings, or when the Jamaica High School baseball team drove out to Alley Pond Park to play against our nemesis, Van Buren, which had its home field there, or against Mid-Queens in the summer league, when I was playing with Joe: *those bars*. Every disreputable joke or rumor I had heard about Creedmoor—as well as the treatment of "the insane," as the mentally ill used to be called—was confirmed by those nightmarish, prison-like bars. I used to shudder when I saw them; all of us did. Never in my wildest dream could I imagine being on the other side of those dreadful bars for any conceivable reason, let alone to visit anyone *I knew*.

And yet that is exactly the incredible reality that presented itself one day in late May, 1968, when I found myself in a car being driven by my close friend and Jamaica teammate Peter Lord, going eastward on Grand Central Parkway as the all-too-familiar main building of Creedmoor loomed into view. Except that *this* time, we weren't headed to Alley Pond Park as the visiting baseball team. I was actually going to visit Creedmoor itself. And, the unseen patient held against her will behind those bars whom I was going to visit was—nightmare of nightmares—my mother.

****

BEFORE continuing to recount my—and my mother's—Creedmoor nightmare, perhaps I should fill you in a little more about who I was when I was sixteen, and in particular what sort of student I was.

Answer: not a very good one. While maintaining respectable grades, I remained largely distracted and unmotivated in school. The lone exception to this depressing status quo was my eleventh grade Social Studies class, taught by a dynamic teacher, Mrs. Lucille Ratkins. She had a flair for getting her sometimes apathetic or otherwise distracted students—like me—to get involved in lively and sometimes passionate discussions of the tumultuous events that were then dominating the front pages of the newspapers and evening news broadcasts, including and especially the Vietnam War, which seemed to be getting worse and worse in the fall and winter of 1967, and the especially tumultuous spring of 1968, which also saw the assassinations of Martin Luther King and Robert Kennedy.

At the same time, Mrs. Ratkins also helped us to place these jarring and unsettling events into some kind of historical context. It was she who first sparked my interest in becoming a Social Studies teacher when I eventually graduated into the "real world," as we called it. She had that rare ability to connect with her students, an ability I would like to think she at least partially passed on to me. If one were to look for the seed of my interest in teaching, the ancient fourth floor room of Jamaica High School, where Mrs. Ratkins—I shall always remember her as Mrs. Ratkins—is a good place to start.

Still, Mrs. Ratkins's brilliance notwithstanding, my head was most decidedly not in my books, nor, for that matter, on current events that epochal year. My passion was for baseball, and specifically for my performance as a pitcher on the Varsity baseball team, where my improving efforts and ability were steadily helping our team advance in the standings while I earned a series of hard-fought victories.

Baseball was more than my passion. It was my buffer, my way of bracing myself against and absorbing the shocks that were emanating from the "real world," as well as the all-too-real and disturbing events that were currently taking place within my own little world, such as the increasing troubles of our second candy store. It was hard not to be distracted by such things.

And yet, when the umpire yelled "play ball" and I was firing away, all was well—at least for the duration of the game. Baseball. That was my overriding passion as the spring term of '68 rolled around, a passion that was rewarded by Coach Sam Pace's increasing confidence in me, as well as a record of 5-0 and my reputation as a good pitcher. I was justly proud of my performance and so was Joe, who was in his usual spot next to the left field foul pole for every home game.

Baseball. That was my passion, as well as my refuge. However, even my beloved baseball proved a poor refuge that spring when my mother had her major breakdown, an event that both totally took me by surprise and shook my world to its foundations.

Not that there had not been warning signs. Her strange behavior pattern first surfaced in late 1959. As I was merely eight years old at the time, I was unaware of what was happening, but I definitely knew something was awry. There was her incessant talking, which rarely made sense, or had any relevance to current events. Gradually, there was an uncharacteristic disregard for her daily responsibilities. Cooking, shopping, and cleaning were sometimes strangely ignored.

Later, when I was ten or eleven, sometimes she would be inexplicably absent from the store when it was her turn to work. Sometimes she would exhibit wild mood swings. Of course I noticed this. Then she would be "normal" again for a while. Every time this happened my father told me not to worry. But of course I knew that he *was* worried.

There was one incident, however, which moved my father to finally to take action. One night in the spring of 1968, my mother was again missing for dinner, only this time, she did not come home until the following afternoon. When she did reappear, she was without our car, and she had no recollection of where it was, or where she had been. Somehow, the police found it a few days later, somewhere in Brooklyn.

39

As was his wont, my father said not to worry. Mom was just going through a bad patch. So I put it out of mind, or tried to, and waited for my mother to work her way through whatever she needed to work through and come back to us, to return to the way she used to be.

****

BUT she never quite did. Or rather, she did, but only after taking a detour through the hell on earth known as Creedmoor.

The longest three days in the history of the Braverman family began on a Monday evening in late May while I was in my room upstairs doing homework—or trying to. As fate would have it, that Thursday I was scheduled to pitch in a home game for our then league-leading Varsity team against our arch nemesis and second place team, Martin Van Buren. Not only would a win against Van Buren—who we had already beaten earlier in the season—be satisfying in and of itself, but it would extend my record to 6-0. Beyond that, a victory would put us in the playoffs and in contention for the city championship and an opportunity for me to play at Yankee Stadium. Yankee Stadium! I had a vision of pitching from the same mound as Whitey Ford. It certainly was a tempting vision.

Imagine that…Yankee Stadium…Still, there was homework to do, and in the back of my mind, of course, I was also worried about my mother. Perhaps, like my father said, she was indeed going through a phase. Surely, she would snap out of it. Anyway, my father seemed to have the situation under control. With a shrug, I returned to my books.

Suddenly, as I was reading, I saw the flashing of lights—red lights—through the Venetian blinds, something we only rarely saw on our quiet inner suburban street. Perhaps, I surmised, someone had been robbed, a rare occurrence in our neighborhood, or there had been an accident of some kind. The latter conjecture was confirmed when I saw an ambulance parked outside—the source of the flashing lights—alongside a police car.

Obviously one of my neighbors had been hurt in some way, I noted with concern.

I also thought I heard some screams.

Strangely, it sounded like those screams were emanating from within our house. Sure enough, as I listened, amazed, the screams were that of my mother, who was downstairs. A struggle of some sort was going on. "I promise to be good! I promise!" my mother was saying. Listening through the door I could make out my father's voice, along with that of someone else. I was too petrified to go see myself. Apparently, my father was trying to cajole my mother to do something, I couldn't tell exactly what. Then—my memory of the horrific event is understandably somewhat jumbled—I heard the sound of someone struggling, obviously my mother.

The next thing I remember, I was peeking out and seeing my mother, enmeshed in a white straitjacket, being forcibly escorted by my father, an ambulance attendant, and one of the policemen who had been summoned—obviously by my father—into the waiting ambulance, while she was fighting and screaming the whole time.

All this, mind you, in full view of our neighbors, which, of course, was the least of my concerns.

My mother…being taken away in a straitjacket…taken away in a *straitjacket*…It was hard to take in. Forty-eight years later, it still is.

But it was true. That deranged woman out there, the one being bundled into that ambulance, was indeed my own mother.

Taken away…

…in a straitjacket…

No, it wasn't true. But it was.

And where were those men taking her?

"To Creedmoor," my father responded, in a trance, after the ambulance with its police escort had disappeared into the night. My father could hardly believe it himself, even though he had made the call.

*To Creedmoor…*I knew my mother was sick, but *Creedmoor?*

41

THUS, two days and a lifetime later, I found myself in the passenger seat of a car driven by Peter Lord, in the eastbound section of Grand Central Parkway. Our destination: Creedmoor State Hospital, as it was then called. It was a Wednesday afternoon. My friend, empathetic beyond his years, was the only one outside of the family whom was entrusted with the knowledge of my mother's enforced hospitalization. Needless to say, of course, he was shocked, though he did his best to hide it as we headed along the parkway to visit my mother...*in there*.

The plan, inasmuch as our shell-shocked family had a plan, was for me to arrive at the hospital first. My father would join me later, after closing the store. That way I would have some time to spend with my mother first. Then we would talk to the doctors about her condition together. That was the plan.

In retrospect, if my father knew the horror show he was sending me into, he probably would have insisted on going first. But what did he know? What did any of us know? It couldn't be *that* bad, could it?

Soon enough—too soon—the all-too-familiar, hulking silhouette of the main hospital building came into view.

And then...we were there.

"Good luck," Peter said, quietly, as I exited the car and headed inside en route to see my mother, somewhere *in there*.

"I'm here to see my mother," I told the admitting attendant in a mechanical voice. He nodded and gave me over to another white-robed staffer, who proceeded to guide me into and through the prison-like maze that is Creedmoor, as he unlocked the first of a series of thick metal doors, each of which banged shut with an increasingly loud thud after we entered the next corridor of hell.

And if this wasn't hell, it certainly was a very convincing facsimile thereof.

****

And hell it certainly was. Mind, this was at a time when "mental wards," as places like Creedmoor were then called, were strictly off limits to the media, nor had there even been many fictionalized portrayals of what went on in Creedmoor or kindred institutions either. The closest that the movie industry had come to a realistic depiction of the horror one might encounter at a mid-twentieth century psychiatric facility was in the late 1940s during Hollywood's brief affair with social realism, most notably in *The Lost Weekend*, Billy Wilder's intense adaptation of the Charles Jackson novel of the same name, about the "lost weekend" of the alcoholic writer, played by Ray Milland. The 1945 film, for which Milland won the Academy Award for Best Actor, included his brief but harrowing detour through the "mental ward" of Bellevue Hospital, with its keening, thrashing inmates. Then there was also the searing *Snake Pit*, the acclaimed 1948 movie starring Olivia de Havilland, about a woman who finds herself in an insane asylum and can't remember how she got there, much of which was actually filmed at an actual California facility, Camarillo State Mental Hospital, and which was so grueling as to spur over a dozen states to institute overdue reforms in their mental facilities.

But, of course, this was long before my time. *One Flew Over the Cuckoo's Nest*, the great 1975 film based on the Ken Kesey novel of that name, about a sane prison inmate by the name of McMurphy who tries to get out of prison by pretending that he is insane and winds up being sent to a fairly realistically portrayed mental asylum of the 1960s. While there, he tries to liven things up for his fellow patients and winds up being lobotomized for his troubles. The film brought back memories of what I had encountered at Creedmoor when I saw it shortly after I had begun my own career as a special education teacher working with special needs children. Even *Cuckoo's Nest*, as frightening as it was, did not, I feel, quite capture the grotesque, *Inferno*-like reality of what I saw during my one, brief, haunting visit to Creedmoor in May, 1968.

In any case, at that time I had nothing to go on, which was probably just as well, because nothing could have prepared me for what I saw and heard (and smelled) that afternoon, as I followed the attendant through those corridors. Not that I saw very much; I was, after all, in a state of shock myself. Nor did I want to see very much. Instinctively, I looked straight ahead, or tried to—the same way one does when one is in a house or place where one should not be.

What I saw was enough. Here and there human forms of indeterminate age were hunched in corners, uttering guttural sounds, apparently with little supervision. None of the inmates—and they really *were* inmates—made eye contact with me, looking down at the stained linoleum floor, or giving a thousand-yard stare. All appeared to be lobotomized (even though that hideous form of "therapy" had thankfully fallen out of usage by then) or hypnotized. My God, I thought, as we advanced through one locked ward after another, doors slamming behind us, how could my mother be expected to recover from her malady, whatever it was, in this *place?* Or, even worse, had she already metamorphosed into one of these *zombies?*

****

IF only…The reality, I discovered to my horror, once we finally reached my mother's bedside, was even worse.

Mom? No…That can't be Mom…that can't be my mother…there must be some mistake…

The semi-comatose woman, lying before me, enveloped in an oxygen tent, was breathing heavily. Her face was pale and swollen.

"That can't be my mother…There must be some mistake…"

There was no mistake, the expressionless nurse assured me.

I looked closer: yes, that was my mother. But why, why was she in this state?

It was difficult enough to find Mom in this horrible place, but to find her in this *state*…It didn't make any sense. When my mother was admitted less than forty-eight hours before, she had been physically fine. What could possibly have transpired during the interim for her to now be in this appalling condition? What was the matter with her *now?*

44

The nurse didn't answer. Instead, after a pause, she indicated that "the doctor"—whoever he was—wished to see me in his office...

This was not just a nightmare. It was getting *worse*. What had happened to my mother? Where had she *gone?*

Once again, I followed the same emotionless attendant, through the same tunnel of terror we had just transited, past the hordes of staring, grunting patients...

Finally, we arrived at the office of doctor "X."

"I'm afraid I have some bad news for you, son," the not unsympathetic physician, a man in his thirties, said, as he looked at my mother's file. "Your mother has leukemia."

"It doesn't look very good," he continued, looking up from the file, leaving me to fill in the rest.

"What?" I said, "My mother has leukemia?" I said (or words to that effect). *She's dying?*

I was staggered: it was simply too much to get my head around. For a moment my mind went blank. Then I thought about my father, who was on the way to the hospital at this moment and was about to meet with the same physician. He had not yet seen Mom. Perhaps just as well...

In a trance, I waited outside the office as my father, looking bewildered, entered...

A moment later I heard my father cry and say something like "Oh no...she's a good woman!" or words to that effect.

I worried about my father's weak heart. How could he handle all this? Exiting the office, he told me to wait there while he went to see Mom...A half an hour later, the two of us, feeling very much like zombies ourselves, were back in the car, heading home. Neither of us said anything to each other, as if saying anything would confirm the awful, unimaginable truth of what we had just learned. Harry said he would call Midge's sister, Mae, in Chicago. Perhaps she could help.

My head was reeling from the shocking revelations of seeing Mom at Creedmoor and learning that she was dying...

Creedmoor...Mom...Leukemia...

It was all a bit too much for a sixteen year old to handle.

45

I tried to focus on what I knew: baseball.

After all, I did have a baseball game to play the following day. Strange days!

****

Amazingly, there was still one more shock to come that head-spinning, stomach-churning day. Fortunately, it was a benign one.

I did not stay in the house when we got home and decided to take a walk to the high school where the baseball team would be in the middle of practice. I watched them from a distance, thinking I was still scheduled to pitch against Van Buren, although that was the last thing on my mind. Pitch? How could I pitch now after receiving this sledgehammer news? I realized how inconsequential everything was, including my beloved baseball, when viewed from the perspective of the news I was just given.

I meandered my way back home. As soon as I entered the house, I knew something had happened because Harry's voice, from a phone conversation I had walked in on, sounded surprisingly upbeat. When he hung up, he explained to me that Midge's sister Mae had called the hospital herself from Chicago, after getting the news about Mom's hospitalization and subsequent diagnosis from Harry.

Amazingly enough, it turned out that there was *another* patient in the hospital named Braverman, who *also* had the first initial M. The doctor had given us a report for that patient, and not my mother! Of course, the realization that the terminal leukemia diagnosis belonged to another real person with a real family tempered my euphoria somewhat.

However, I was sixteen years old, and I had just been told my mother had received what seemed like a cosmic pardon. I took it. The truth was that my mother had contracted *pneumonia*—not leukemia. Hence the oxygen tent and her sickly appearance.

I thought the sooner she got out of that place, the better. My mother's mistaken diagnosis obviously had not enhanced our confidence in the institution.

46

The shock of seeing my mother taken away in a straitjacket...visiting Creedmoor...seeing Mom lying there...learning that she had leukemia...now finding out that she *didn't* have leukemia...talk about a roller-coaster...

I was numb. So was my father. At least, we felt, Mom *would* be coming back to us.

But when?

I went out for another walk. Slowly but surely, my pulverized thoughts began to sort themselves out.

OK...Mom doesn't have leukemia...She'll be ok...We'll be ok...

What a day. I allowed myself my first smile in seventy-two hours.

Then I remembered: I'm supposed to pitch tomorrow. I began focusing on the game.

You'll be ok, I assured myself. *You'll be ok...*

And I began thinking about what I had been thinking three days before, before the Venetian blinds in my bedroom had lit up with those flashing lights and my world had fallen in: I began fantasizing how I was going to strike out the other side the next day and win The Big Game and just maybe go on to play in Yankee Stadium.

****

UNFORTUNATELY, it didn't quite happen that day. Close, but not quite. But *oh* so close.

Like all of the games I pitched, either for Jamaica High or for Joe Austin—not to mention the thousands more I went on to coach during my subsequent coaching career—I can remember that now nearly half-a-century-ago game against Van Buren as if it were yesterday.

Did I get my focus back? Well, I tried. I stayed home from school the next day, with my father's blessing, something I didn't do very often, to help me get my game face on. Obviously, it was hard to put the events of the past twenty-four hours out of mind, but I tried. Above all, I didn't want to let my teammates down. Although Coach Pace—obviously—knew that there was something wrong with my mother, in retrospect I doubt that he would have asked me to start if he had known the facts; I certainly wouldn't have asked or expected any high school junior kid who had experienced the rollercoaster I had just gone through to start.

Of course, intense competitor that I was, I wouldn't have had it any other way. Unsurprisingly, my stomach was churning when I finally took the mound that memorable afternoon at Jamaica, and the umpire cried "Play ball!" As usual, Joe, my mentor and godfather, was in the sizable—and vocal—home field crowd that day, as he was for every home game, taking his favorite spot near the left field foul pole.

So was Roger, who was standing considerably closer, along with the rest of my Jamaica friends, including the aforementioned Jimmy Gonedes, of insect farm fame, my best friend, Billy Rappaport, and several other encouraging fans.

In fact, I later learned that Roger, who of course knew a thing or two about the game, was close enough to call all of my pitches, even though I was completely unaware of it at the time! Not that this helped. Well, maybe it helped. After all, I *almost* won.

When the game finally commenced, I was clearly pressing. Every inning was a struggle to find my rhythm and command. I did not feel I had my good stuff, but miraculously, I averted disaster, and by the bottom of the sixth we were only trailing 3-2. I have always thought the last of the sixth is an especially precarious frame for the visiting team clinging to a small lead. Perhaps that belief originated in that milestone (at least for me) game.

The Jamaica Beavers were attempting to rally for the tying score and had runners on first and second with two out. It was time for our clutch shortstop and captain, Peter—the same Peter who had driven me to Creedmoor State Hospital the day before —to take center stage. Peter, who had been slumping of late, had been put in the eighth spot by Coach Pace. Maybe, we hoped, Peter would come through with a single for us and knock in the tying run.

Well, to make a long story short, Peter did better than that—much better. Watching the ball intently, the steady infielder let a couple of pitches go by. Then—*WHAM!*—the next thing we knew, the ball was, to paraphrase a popular song of the day, soaring up, up, and away, over the fence and across the street, crashing against the side of Thomas Edison Vocational on one bounce. Score: Jamaica 5, Van Buren 3.

Or to paraphrase the late great Yankee shortstop and announcer Phil Rizzuto, HOLY COW!

Holy Cow indeed! As the ball sailed over the fence, Coach Pace and his volunteer assistant, Mike Becker, who also happened to be a Mets scout, turned to each other and shook hands. Roger proclaimed free ice cream sodas at Harry and Midge's Candy Store. Peter Lord, who never got recognition, had come through big time. I was the only subdued person on our side as Peter crossed the plate with our fifth run, for I knew there were still three more outs to be recorded in the seventh.

****

THOSE three outs proved as hard to get as I feared. With the score now 5-3, Van Buren was sending their eighth, ninth, and first hitters to the plate. My struggle in the first six innings continued when I walked the leadoff hitter. After bouncing a curveball in the dirt, which allowed the runner to advance to second, I was able to strike out the number nine hitter. The next batter tapped the ball weakly up the first base line, and I carefully underhanded the ball to first baseman Mike Schwartz, for the second out. I was just one out away from a league championship and a spot in the city playoffs.

Van Buren's number two hitter (whose name escapes me), who was hitless against me in the two games that season, was now up at bat. He had had a lot of trouble with my breaking ball (which Roger was obviously aware of, because he kept calling that pitch—via the catcher, of course!). Early in the count another curve went in the dirt, advancing the runner to third.

49

With the count 2-2 I decided to close out the deal with a curve ball down and in.

Unfortunately, the baseball gods were not with me. My following pitch broke too far down and in and hit the batter, putting the tying run on base, with the go ahead run coming to the plate.

A costly mistake. Now I would have to contend with Van Buren's best hitter, the formidable Mike Bergman. Bergman, a strapping righty, had always been a tough out for me.

Now I made another mistake—a break in concentration. Given the hitter, and the situation, I should have tried to set up the runner on first for a pickoff. I had a decent pick off move, thanks to the practice with it I had had with Roger, and with runners on first and third, and the trailing runner the potential tying run, a steal attempt was likely.

Instead, my blood up, I decided to face down Bergman and forgot the runner at first. Mistake. After Bergman fouled off my first pitch, a fastball, the runner took advantage of my next pitch, a low curve, and with a huge jump, easily beat catcher Bobby Sacca's throw to second. There were now runners on second and third. The formerly raucous home field crowd, sensing that the furies had turned against us, grew tense and quiet. Even my self-anointed pitching coach, Roger, piped down as my duel with the mighty Bergman reached its inexorable climax.

I was fleetingly aware of the fact that I had reached one of the defining moments of my life, and I imagine so was Bergman. The towering Van Buren batsman was just a swing away from revising the game; I, the relatively diminutive pitcher of Jamaica, was just a pitch away from nailing the game, steering our team into the city playoffs and bringing me one step closer to achieving my lifelong dream of pitching in Yankee Stadium.

All this less than a day after visiting my involuntarily committed mother and learning that she was about to die, then just as soon learning of her seemingly cosmic stay of execution. Talk about pressure…How I was able to hold it together I don't know.

Looking on from shortstop, Peter—the only one on the field who knew just how much I was dealing with at that moment—was willing me on. I could almost hear him under my breath, exhorting me on to victory, a victory that would also be his.

Come on Jesse…Come on Jesse! Strike the guy out!

After the three straight fastballs failed to get past Bergman, I decided to try a curve, visualizing the ball dipping under his bat for the climatic out. I reached back to snap off my best breaking ball. The crowd held its breath…and

Bang! There the ball went. A grounder, I thought. *Good.* But Bergman had hit the ball too hard. It eluded the second baseman. Bergman had his clutch single. A moment later, the score was tied, as the runner on second base just made it to home plate, beating the throw to Bobby Sacca, while Bergman, quick to take advantage, took second on the throw, as the crowd groaned.

It was now five to five. Two outs. Van Buren had the go-ahead run on second, with one of its top hitters, the tall and imposing Dennis Lacina, coming up to bat. Earlier in the season the towering lefty had hit a tape measure home run off me. It didn't look good.

I reached back again. The crowd again held its breath. This time Lacina timed his swing perfectly, swatting a frozen rope to right field, as the go-ahead run came in. Six to five. I managed to get the next batter out, but I was disconsolate as I walked to the bench.

Three short outs later it was over. Game to Van Buren. Close, oh so close. But no cigar. And so, the Jamaica Beavers' dream, and mine, of playing in Yankee Stadium and reaching eternal baseball glory, had died.

Nearly a half century after that heart-stopping afternoon, I still sometimes chide myself for not trying to pick off that runner on first. The wonder, of course, was that I had done as well as I had. But that was of little solace as I tucked my glove under my arm and headed home. Roger, no less dejected than I, patted me on the back and told me how proud he was of me, but I didn't hear him. All I knew was that I had lost.

Thus ended perhaps the most dramatic—and traumatic—twenty hours of my life.

****

SEVERAL WEEKS later Midge finally came home from Creedmoor. My memory of her homecoming is not clear. It may have been a couple of months, I don't know. By then, it was summer and with the Jamaica season over, I was back in the secure feeling of playing for Joe.

I don't think I ever discussed my mother's ordeal with Joe, but I suspect he knew. Anyway, it wouldn't have been like him to say anything. That wasn't Joe. The key thing was that Joe was there. Of course, we Emeralds knew, Joe, now in his late sixties, would not always be there, but that didn't matter. For the moment, he was still there, every morning, as he had been forever, scraping and kicking the field into shape, ready to play ball, and that was good enough for me.

Who needed summer camp when we had Joe? Who cared that the country, no less the world, was in the midst of blowing itself up, as we could readily see that summer on the network news, as the horrendous images of the Chicago Police swatting away at the demonstrators who were protesting the Democratic Convention and other assorted cataclysms played across the screen of our living room television set.

Anyway, there was still enough to worry about at home.

My mother? She never recovered, really. The ordeal of her involuntary admission was never discussed, but it hung heavily in the air. I sensed that she was hurt by Harry and Roger's decision to commit her to Creedmoor, but we never talked about that. She was still too fragile. She was able to resume her duties at home and at the store, but only with difficulty. Dad, for his part, was just happy to have her home again. Meanwhile, he still had his troubles holding the store together. In this respect, he wasn't really there for me (as much as he would have liked to be). It was basically a sad time.

Roger, for his part, was also otherwise preoccupied. Having outgrown his self-described "beach bum" phase, he was now back in school at Long Island University, studying hard, while working nights at the post office in order to pay for his tuition. Harry, like most other parents of that day and age who had grown up during the Depression and the Second World War, held little truck with restless youth, including and especially if one was his own son. He had given Roger an ultimatum. If he wanted to go back to school, fine, but he would have to pay his own way through. And so, to his credit, he did.

But Roger, for the most part, kept his head down when he came home, closing the door and losing himself in his books and his transistor radio. Also, the seven-year difference in our ages—I was, after all, still a teenager, while Roger was well into his twenties—couldn't be denied. He was still around to cheer me on the field, as well as for the occasional game of ping-pong on the table set in the basement, but, for all practical purposes, he wasn't there either.

****

ONE person who *was* there for me during my late wonder years, so to speak, and who to some degree filled the role of mentor and older brother for me was another one of "Joe's boys," an intellectually oriented athlete and a close neighbor of mine by the name of Bruce Lerro. I had long been a fan of Bruce, who was three years my senior and had begun as a second baseman for the "older" Emeralds, before seamlessly making the conversion to center field. I well remember the graceful way he would lope across the outfield, snag a seemingly sure-to-drop fly ball, and make it look easy.

Because we were three years apart in age, we didn't have much of a chance to actually play baseball with each other, but Bruce and I did spend a lot of time together at his house playing "virtual baseball" (as it would be called today) on the realistic board game then popular with the urban teen set known as "APBA." We also played a lot of touch football. One of my favorite ways of blowing off steam when I wasn't in school or on the mound was tossing the pigskin around with my talented neighbor.

Bruce and I also spent a great deal of time together watching sports, particularly basketball. Twice a week throughout my high school years, my adoptive older brother and I would head off to Madison Square Garden to watch the Knicks play.

However, our favorite shared activity, I think, was simply *talking,* though not so much about our respective problems or issues. No, what we liked to talk about was what *was behind things,* what made *things tick,* especially sports. Whenever Bruce and I were together, we would dissect every play of the baseball or touch football game we had just had. Strategies that worked as well as those that didn't were rehashed until every element of the strategy we had used, or not used, was exhausted.

But that was just the start. Then, with this self-styled athlete-intellectual leading the way, we would pull the cameras back, so to speak, and talk about sports in general, including the athletic or "jock" subculture we seemed to have become swept up in. We would talk about the psychology of it, the sociology of it—this, mind you, before either of us had even read a book of sociology. I don't even think either of us knew what the word "sociology" really meant.

Basically, of course, we just talked. But it was fun, as well as comforting to have someone to do that with, especially when things at home were getting difficult. Like my other close friends, Bruce was sensitive, caring, loyal, and empathetic, and we just seemed to be on a similar "wavelength."

****

ANOTHER friend who was there for me during the difficult days following my mother's breakdown, and who always has been there for me, was Billy Rappaport, my oldest and dearest friend.

To be sure, although we might have seemed unlikely comrades to some—inasmuch as I was the (much) better-behaved of us (by far), as well as the better student—Bill and I had much in common. For one, we lived just two blocks away from each other. For another, we both loved sports.

And both of us shared the searing experience of having a close relative—in Billy's case, his brother Joey—who had psychological problems—except that in Bill's case, the experience was even more searing and continuous, as well as deleterious to his own emotional and mental health, leading him to "act out" (as the expression went) and cause problems with his teachers and classmates.

To be sure, anyone who encountered the younger Bill, particularly during his childhood and early adolescent years, might well have pegged him as a "juvenile delinquent." Or "J.D." as aggressive, maladjusted students were labeled (and mislabeled) in those post-"Asphalt Jungle" days. My coauthor, who served at P.S. 131 as Captain of the Hall Monitors, a title that came with a badge and the power to "step out" any student who was acting out of line, i.e., to ask him (or her) to stand against the wall for the remainder of the lunchtime recess, remembers Bill as one of his most frequent offenders.

Similarly, most of Bill's teachers at 131 and Van Wyck Junior High pegged him as a "troublemaker" or worse. Inattentive, openly disrespectful of his teachers, and quick to take umbrage at real or perceived slights, the brash, clearly maladjusted youngster seemed headed for a problematic future to say the least.

And most likely, he was. His manifestly high I.Q., as evidenced on the occasional standardized tests he managed to sit still for, was simply ignored.

In fact, everyone—except for me, the only person who knew the "real" Bill—got Bill wrong, something which I would take strongly into account in my future career as a special education teacher when I was handed similar "troublemakers."

What Bill's teachers and peers—as well as my esteemed coauthor—didn't see, or didn't wish to see, or simply couldn't, was the "other" Bill, the empathetic Bill, the selfless Bill, the easygoing Bill, as well as the preternaturally bright Bill; the Bill who was my best friend and closest confidante (and still is); and

55

the Bill who would eventually become the Dr. William Rappaport, General Surgeon, of today.

Also, what they didn't see—or only saw the "tip" of—or misdiagnosed altogether (another common experience to our families), was the extraordinary, really overwhelming situation Bill was facing at home, in the person of his *truly* disturbed brother, Joe, who would act the savant idiot one moment—recounting abstruse details of astronomy and the like—and then do something obviously inappropriate the next.

Clearly, something was "wrong" with Joey. The word around the neighborhood was that he was "mentally retarded," the then catchall and stigmatizing phrase for anyone who was "not normal." As we know now—and as he was eventually (and correctly) diagnosed—Joe was autistic and schizophrenic.

Unsurprisingly, Joe's malady, and the pain and embarrassment of having to cope with and explain his brother's seemingly irrational behavior, had an effect on Bill. Compounding and aggravating the situation for Bill was his despairing parents' confused and contradictory reaction to their elder son's behavior, and differing opinions about the best treatment for their son.

Unaware of the true nature of Joe's illness, Bill's mother apparently believed that sweet reasonableness was the way to go; that Joe would get better, eventually, if only he was shown enough love and understanding.

Bill's father was a doctor, which one might think might have made him more sympathetic to his son's condition, but in fact just the opposite was true. Evidently Dr. Rappaport leaned toward committing Joe to Creedmoor—the same purgatory where my mother eventually "did time," which in turn further distressed his mother. Put simply, it was not a happy home.

Meanwhile, Bill was still left with having to deal with the stigma, embarrassment, and confusion of being the brother of "crazy Joey."

The aggressive, antisocial behavior that his teachers and schoolmates saw was the inevitable result of this dreadful situation. Unfortunately, they didn't realize that. They only saw the behavior. I, of course, knew better. I was the only one who knew the "other" Bill, the Bill who was my warm, empathetic, funny and intelligent friend. Of course, I didn't know or understand the full details of the turmoil he was going through at home, but it was pretty obvious that he was having problems.

I also saw something else—although this should have been readily apparent to anyone who saw Bill's wan and fluctuating physical appearance. At some point in his early teens, Bill developed a painful and chronic inflammation of the gastrointestinal tract. Known—or now known—as Crohn's Disease, this dreadful malady causes severe stomach aches, diarrhea, and weight loss, all of which Bill suffered from. Although there is no way of proving this, Bill's conflicted home situation was almost certainly a contributing factor, if not the principal contributing factor to the disease.

Little wonder—and mind, this was still in the day when most teachers had little or no serious grounding in either psychiatric or medical issues—that Bill acted the way he did. Or that he took refuge in and comfort from my friendship, as I did in his. Indeed, if there was anyone amongst the few friends to whom I confided my own mother's psychological problems who could imagine the uproar and dislocation which her grievous situation caused and were causing in our home, it was Bill. Others could intuit. But Bill *knew*.

In fact, now that I think about it, one could say that this, Bill's and my respective experiences of "the dark side" (so to speak), was another tie that bound us, though by no means the most important one. Of course, even though I loved Bill and was his best friend, there was only so much that I could do to help him with his problems at school. And he *was* having problems at school. For years, when we were in the same class, Bill would make a habit of calling me, his "law-abiding," teacher-fearing friend, to ask for that day's homework assignment. Not that I minded.

Then, he wouldn't do it. That was OK by me, of course; however, invariably, his teachers weren't as philosophical, particularly when he didn't show up at all and continued to wind up spending time "stepped out" against the wall by Captain Sander, or, at Van Wyck, in Detention Room.

For all I knew, Bill *was* headed for a bad way (as they used to say). In fact, at one point, when he was thirteen or fourteen, and we were both at Van Wyck, and his unexplained absences from school were accruing, it wasn't clear whether he would actually graduate. I was worried about Bill. Who, knowing everything he was dealing with or going through, including his new physical affliction, wouldn't be? Still somehow, knowing Bill's true character, I had faith that somehow things would get better for Bill, that somehow he would turn himself around, a faith, I might say, that absolutely no one else, except his long-suffering mother, shared.

And that, to make a long story short, is exactly what happened. Of course, as his friend and confidante, I always knew how bright he was. That didn't surprise me. But still, I have to admit, I was pretty taken aback by the suddenness with which Bill was hitting the books. Years later, Bill confided to me that a certain substitute teacher at Jamaica helped spark his turnaround. But of course it was mostly his doing.

I have to say, in retrospect, I have rarely if ever seen quite so sudden or dramatic a turnaround as Bill effected between the ages of fourteen and fifteen. At any rate, Bill certainly wasn't calling me for the homework anymore!

By the time he and I entered Jamaica High in 1966, Bill the juvenile delinquent had completely given way to Bill-the-A-student-with-the-bright-future. This for someone who at one point most knowledgeable observers had predicted had no future at all, no less who would be studying hard for his SATs!

So much for "incorrigible!" Eventually, Bill applied to and was accepted to the estimable University of Miami, where he wound up achieving a 3.96 cumulative average, graduated in three years, and was offered immediate admission to Miami's medical school. Talk about turning new leaves!

****

I WISH I could say that I effected as dramatic a turnaround in my studies as Bill, however although I did well in some of my courses, especially Social Studies and History, the best I can say about my own academic performance at Jamaica was that it better than average—but certainly less than one would expect from someone who would eventually devote himself to a career in teaching and effecting turnarounds similar to Bill's.

I did manage to gain admission to several excellent colleges, including a few which had expressed possible interest in my playing baseball for them, and eventually decided on one of these, the University of Bridgeport, in Bridgeport, Connecticut, where I seemed fairly sure of gaining a slot with their Varsity baseball team.

In the meantime, I had begun my final season pitching for the Jamaica Beavers, an experience that was largely an anticlimactic one.

Unfortunately, the season resulted in a disappointing 7 – 7 record, compared to our 10 – 4 record of the year before. My efforts to put the previous year's heartbreaking defeat to Van Buren behind me were not completely successful, and I continued to play that game over and again in my imagination. It seemed that loss had threatened my confidence.

****

Nevertheless, the season was not a total washout. For one, I managed to hit my first home run in a game I pitched, a home game early in the season against top rival Benjamin Cardozo, thanks to my new secret weapon: a cracked major league bat that Bobby Sacca, who in the meantime had gotten a job as a batboy for the Mets, had given me, and which Joe helped me carefully tape and repair, before giving it back to me with a wink.

Unfortunately, my amazing hit was in a losing cause. The imposing Cardozo lineup, including precisionist southpaw pitcher Ken Moisoff and hard-hitting first baseman Ricky Sposta, both of whom would go on to have strong collegiate careers, at NYU and Seton Hall, respectively, were just too good. We wound up

59

losing the game, while Cardozo, energized by their victory over us, went on a hot streak, winning the next seven games in a row and leaving us and their other competitors in the dust.

Still, that homer was a rare thrill for me. The ball, which barely cleared the fence right down the line, was also aided by a strong wind blowing from right to left. I'll never forget that.

Even more satisfyingly, I belatedly discovered and corrected my "telegraphing" problem, allowing me, six weeks later, to cap the season, as well as my high school Varsity baseball career, with a sweet victory—against Cardozo no less. After too many losses that season, I finally realized that I was adjusting my grip on the ball inside my glove every time I prepared to throw a curve, thus negating my best pitch. Apparently, this inadvertent signal had become common knowledge in the league.

Well, I quickly did something about that. This time I decided to call my own game and decide on my own which pitch to throw, depriving the enemy of his early warning Braverman detection system, and leaving him once again vulnerable to my trademark pitch. Suddenly, once again, the opposing hitters were swinging helplessly at my curve as it broke and dipped across the plate. Or they were frozen, like deer in the headlights, by my fastball, which they took on the outside corner, when they were thinking that the curve was coming. Or they would just swing at it feebly, as the formidable Sposta did on one particularly enjoyable at bat.

Suddenly, for one last delicious May afternoon, to the delight and relief of my fellow Beavers, I was back to my old form. Once again, I could feel the excitement of winning a big game.

"Hey," I could sense the Jamaicans in the crowd nudging each other appreciably as I retired the Cardozans one scoreless inning after another. *Jesse is back!*

And so I was, for that last memorable game against Cardozo. When the last Cardozo hitter flied out to left, the score stood as follows:

JAMAICA: 4

CARDOZO: 1

I had actually pitched a two hitter.

The season may have fallen far short of a junior year encore, but with this successful final game, I regained my confidence and hope for the summer and the college years to come. It almost made up for the crushing defeat of the previous year against Van Buren, and my vanished dream of pitching in Yankee Stadium.

Almost, but not quite.

****

ACTUALLY, as the fickle furies had it, that star-crossed year of 1969, as America entered the first year of the Nixon era, the war in Vietnam continued to drag on, and the counterculture reached an apotheosis of sorts at the Woodstock Music Festival—events I was of course aware of, if not directly affected by—I *did* have the chance to rub elbows with some New York major leaguers.

I even got a chance to run down balls in a major league stadium, while having a ringside seat to one of the most memorable—I should say *amazing*—stories in recent baseball history. Except that the major leaguers in question weren't the Yankees, but rather that other formerly woebegone team from the other side of the city—*my* side of the city.

I'm talking about the New York Mets, of course. The stadium was the late, great Shea Stadium, just a short subway ride away in Flushing, Queens. The remarkable story I witnessed for two—really one—game, was, of course, the formerly laughable Mets' transformation into the Amazing Mets of 1969.

As those of you who are old enough can recall, for the first part of the 1969 major league baseball season, it had appeared that the story of the year would be that of the long-suffering Chicago Cubs, who appeared poised to end two decades of frustration. Yet just beneath them in their own National League East Division, the once buffoonish New York Mets were building a Cinderella story of their own.

As the Mets continued to climb in the standings, the Cubs' Ron Santo expressed his befuddlement at the Mets' winning ways. "I know the Dodgers won pennants with just pitching, but this

Mets lineup is ridiculous," he ranted. "It's a shame losing to an infield like that," he said of one lineup that had featured Ed Kranepool, Wayne Garrett, Al Weis and Bobby Pfiel—none of whom even hit .240 that year.

The reason I was able to have a ringside seat to the Mets' remarkable ascent is that on two occasions that memorable year, my former JHS friend, Bobby Sacca, who had since graduated and had managed to snag the enviable job of batboy with the Mets, invited me to take his place.

In the event, the superstitious Mets players, for whom Bobby was a sort of good luck charm, and who didn't take lightly to having a new face in the dugout, promptly dismissed me, demoting me to the role of ball boy, assigned the somewhat less glamorous mission of fetching foul balls and errant line drives hit in their direction. That was fine by me. Just being on the field in uniform was a sufficient thrill. Of course, I would have preferred "playing" in Yankee Stadium, but you can't have everything.

Anyway, the Yankees, now sans the mighty bats and arms that had won them all those pennants and World Series in the 1950s and early 60s (1968 was also Mickey Mantle's last season)—Casey Stengel's Yankees—had not been in serious contention for half a decade, nor would they be for another half decade, when the next generation of Yankees, George Steinbrenner's Yankees, began to get cooking. In the meantime, the Mets *were* in contention and that was exciting to see. Particularly because it was, you know, the Mets, the same team that all of us had poked fun at during the seven seasons since their inception.

Now, suddenly, the old "Meet the Mets, Beat the Mets!" Mets were the *Amazing* Mets.

How did one account for this seemingly preternatural phenomenon?

A major factor, of course, was the practical, can-do management style of Stengel and Wes Westrum's successor as manager, Gil Hodges, a six-foot-two former marine sergeant with a pastor's face and a head for baseball, whose platoon system produced favorable lefty-righty matchups that yielded deceptively productive results, most notably in right field, where the right-handed Ron Swoboda and his left-handed alternate, Art Shamsky, combined to produce an impressive 99 RBI from that position. In much the same way, the left-handed Ed Kranepool and the right-handed Donn Clendenon, a mid-season acquisition from the Montreal Expos, gave the Mets a power-hitting duo at first base, while skillful hitter Ken Boswell and crack glove man Al Weis took turns at second base.

I also was impressed by Hodges's Austin-like resolution, which he displayed most memorably on July 30, in the second game of a doubleheader against the Astros, after the Astros, in a moment that brought back memories of the old Mets, had managed to score ten runs against the Mets in the second inning. During that outburst, outfielder Cleon Jones (who was nursing an injury), gingerly chased a double into the corner by catcher Johnny Edwards and tossed it lackadaisically back into the infield.

Following that play, which I later saw on television, Hodges barged out of the dugout, and instead of stopping at the mound for a pitching change, as everyone expected, continued past the mound, past the shortstop, and out to Jones in left field. The Shea crowd saw the two men exchange words. If Hodges didn't say, "If you don't want to play ball get off the field," he sure as hell said something like it. A few moments later, the crowd watched as Hodges escorted a sullen Jones to the dugout.

"I saw him favor his leg that inning," the self-effacing Hodges later explained to *The New York Times*. "I didn't think he should play if he was hurting." But of course what he was really doing was sending a message to the team. Jones, for his part, certainly got it. "It might have looked like he was trying to embarrass me," the left fielder later put it. "But it wasn't. Gil was just trying to make a point. We were getting our asses kicked and something had to be done, and that was his way of showing us that he wasn't satisfied with the way we were playing."

The other secret of the Mets' newfound success, besides Hodges's brainy management style, was, of course, their pitching. While the Mets' bats fell into periodic slumps, the team's pitching staff was consistently strong and frequently great throughout the year. In the team's 162 regular season games that year, Mets arms held their opponents to two runs or less an amazing ninety-two games. Leading the staff was twenty-four-year-old hurler Tom Seaver, who in 1969 took that next step from being a promising young pitcher to being "The Franchise." In perhaps the best season of his Hall of Fame career, Seaver won twenty-five games while losing only seven, allowing 2.21 earned runs a game. The Mets' ace lived up to the role of a stopper—the guy who takes the mound and gets it done when his team needs it the most.

Now, in August, when I worked my second game, the Mets were in the midst of a glory run of their own, a ten-game home stand which would see them take nine out of ten and ultimately overtake the sagging Cubs, and it was an exciting—nay amazing—thing to behold, particularly if you happened to be on the field itself, just a few feet away from the action. In addition to giving me a deeper understanding of the Mets' on-field talents, my stint as ballboy also increased my appreciation for that other undeniable element of the Mets' surprising success: their passionate fans, who were leading the National League in both attendance and demonstrativeness, and all of whom seemed to be breathing down my neck when they weren't busy razzing me.

"Ah, tomorrow you'll be selling hot dogs!" I remember one deranged fan shouting at me when I failed to snare one line drive hit in my direction during the second game I worked, against the Braves, knocking the ball down with my chest instead of snaring it with my glove. Didn't matter to me, I was a star, and all the fans asking me for my autograph proved it. Even though my heart still belonged to the Yankees, on that day, as well as that amazing summer, which would culminate with the Mets beating the Baltimore Orioles four games to one in the World Series, it was on loan to the Amazing Mets.

I even picked up a valuable tip from Mets catcher J.C. Martin, who suggested using a "phony" head shake when throwing a 0-2 pitch. According to Martin, when hitters saw a pitcher shaking off their catcher's sign on a 0-2 count, they tend to think that some sort of experimental off-speed pitch is coming. Therefore, the friendly catcher advised during one of the pregame warm-ups, throw the fastball when the batter was least expecting it. Duly noted!

And then, before I knew it, the summer was over, and I was saying my tearful farewell to my parents and the world I knew, including our stalwart, if fading, Flushing candy store, my brother Roger, Joe, and my Emeralds friends, and I was packing my things, most notably my cherished baseball glove, into the family car, and I was off to Bridgeport and the next chapter of my life, and, I was confident, the next stage of my baseball career.

Unfortunately, it turned out, I was wrong about that.

CHAPTER 4:
THE GREENING OF JESSE BRAVERMAN

I can see clearly now the rain has gone
I can see all obstacles in my way
Gone are the dark clouds that had me blind
It's gonna be a bright, bright sun shiny day

—"I Can See Clearly Now" by Johnny Nash

I MAY not have been a member of Woodstock Nation, or close to one, but I have to admit I certainly was feeling pretty groovy that long ago day in September, 1969 when I piled into the family car with my father for the one-and-a-half-hour drive to go off to Bridgeport to start my new life as a college student.

And a new life it certainly would be. Unlike many, if not most, of my classmates and peers, I had never gone to sleepaway camp or vacationed abroad. Indeed, in my entire life, I had never spent more than a few nights away from home. Bridgeport may only have been sixty-five miles away from Jamaica, but for all practical purposes that car trip was the equivalent of a moon shot for me.

Like any normal college freshman, let alone anyone who had never been away from home, I was understandably anxious about the next chapter of my life. How would I like Bridgeport? After all, I had never visited the sprawling seaside Connecticut campus, although it certainly looked nice from the pamphlets I had seen. How would I like my fellow college students? And most importantly, how would I be able to compete in baseball?

These were some of the questions and concerns I had as we zoomed off to Planet Bridgeport. Naturally, I was also concerned about my long-suffering mother; I still remember her standing in the doorway of our house saying goodbye with a rather forlorn look. How I hated to leave her.

Nevertheless, she knew—*I* knew—it was time. Anyway, I would be back for Thanksgiving!

Although my father certainly had his worries, including our now-failing and soon-to-close Flushing candy store, as well as my mother's health (not to mention his own), he never let on to these. As far as I was concerned, his principal wish was that I would use my college experience to make a good life for myself—and hopefully an easier one than he had had.

Hopefully, too, I would also get a career out of the experience. Toward that end, inspired in part by the memory of Mrs. Ratkins, as well as some of the other better teachers I had had at Van Wyck and Jamaica, I had declared a major in secondary education, with a minor in history.

Still, Jesse Braverman being Jesse Braverman, the main thing on my mind, once I wished my father a tearful goodbye and sent him off with a big hug, was when I would get back to the diamond. Toward that end, one of the first things I did after I had moved into my assigned room in North Hall, the standard issue dormitory to which I was assigned, and introduced myself to my roommate, a friendly guy by the name of Stu Abramson, was to hasten across the tree-covered campus to the university athletic offices to check in with Tom Whalen, the same coach who had encouraged me to come to Bridgeport to pitch for his well-regarded Purple Knights, and see when my first workout would be.

Hence my surprise when my enthusiastic knock on the Varsity Coach's door was answered not by Coach Whalen, but his successor, a tough, crew-cut customer by the name of Fran Bacon whom I had never met before or heard of.

Unsurprisingly, Coach Bacon, who had only just replaced the departed Whalen and was just getting acquainted with his new surroundings and charges, hadn't heard of me or my athletic achievements either, nor did he know anything about his predecessor's effort to recruit me. *That* was something of a downer. Here I was all set to get off to a fast head start on my collegiate baseball career and the head coach didn't even know who I was.

Instead, Bacon simply remarked that he would take a look at me at the start of the next term, in January, when the preseason workouts began. Not a good sign, I thought as I excused myself and trotted disconsolately back to my room...

Nevertheless, shrugging off my disappointment, I resolved to impress Bacon and prepare myself for my first season on the mound for the Purple Knights. And so I did, taking long jogs along the beach at Seaside Park by the Long Island Sound that fall and winter in order to be in top shape for when the first workouts began. In between runs, I studied, made a few friends, and while not participating myself, took note of the growing anti-war demonstrations. I also made a conscious decision not to participate in fraternity life, which dominated the Bridgeport campus at the time: not my style.

Above all, my focus was on playing baseball. Intellectually, of course, I knew that there were bigger and stronger athletes and potential college players on campus. Nevertheless I was confident that I would make the cut when the time came. In the meantime I bided my time and adjusted to college life as best as I could.

Still, nothing could have prepared me for that first workout in January, 1970 and seeing the giants I would be competing with—strapping, prehensile monsters who ranged as tall as six foot six and looked to weigh at least fifty to ninety pounds more than me.

I also was astonished to see the speeds at which the pitchers were able to throw, and the bat speed of the hitters. It made me wonder whether even my determination was sufficient to overcome these physical mismatches.

Finally, on a cool damp day in March, on a makeshift field near the varsity diamond, which was still unplayable because of the blustery weather, the baseball roster candidates assembled for our "audition" with the gimlet-eyed Coach Bacon and his assistants, an intra-squad game in which we would showcase our relative talents. This was my chance.

Or so I thought. Several innings passed by before I was told to warm up: evidently Bacon didn't expect very much of me. I would show them, I said to myself as my usual pre-game jitters disappeared and the old adrenaline began pumping.

Sure enough, I disposed of my first hitter on three straight strikes. I still had my stuff.

Then up came the next batter. Curveball. Strike one. Breaking ball. Whiff! Strike two. Fastball. Strike three! I had my second out. I had yet to pitch a ball. I could sense that Bacon and his assistants were beginning to take notice. Things were definitely going my way.

Not so fast.

Next up came one of Bridgeport's toughest hitters, a formidable fellow by the name of Craig Scalzo, who proceeded to foul off five straight of my pitches, before drawing a walk. I was beginning to slip.

Now I had to deal with the Knights' top batsman, third baseman Ron DeFeo. I was determined not to walk him, as I had Scalzo. I decided to challenge him with a fastball.

DeFeo took a swing, crushing it—*boom!*—and sending the ball zooming in the direction of Long Island Sound, and with it my hopes of pitching for the Bridgeport varsity baseball team. In the event, I didn't throw another pitch that fateful afternoon. I didn't need to. In one fell swoop—literally—my dream was over. Despite all of my successes playing for Joe and Jamaica, I knew, as I made my way back to my room and flopped on the bed, a college baseball career was probably beyond my reach. As the saying goes, I had hit the wall.

It was, unquestionably, one of the most depressing moments of my life. I felt that I had failed. Up until that point baseball had been pretty much my main reason for being.

Now, all of a sudden, it was gone.

It wasn't completely gone. I knew that I probably could still play for the Bridgeport junior varsity—as I ultimately did, for two seasons—but I also knew my glory days as Jesse the star pitcher were definitely over. If I wanted to define myself in college, I would have to find another way of doing it.

And so I did by finding a new love—the theater—and triumphing in the part of a flaming "homosexual" queen!

Life is strange! *Stay tuned!*

****

IT all began with a movie. Or rather it began with a job. In the summer of 1970, following my freshman year, I took a job as an usher at the Parsons Theater on Parsons Boulevard in Flushing, just north of Union Turnpike. If I had had my druthers I would have just continued playing for Joe, but I needed to make some money, and working as an usher seemed a good way of doing it.

One of the movies being screened that summer was the then-sensational *The Boys in the Band*. Based on the hit 1968 off-Broadway play of the same name by Mart Crowley, *The Boys*, briefly, revolves around a birthday party that Michael, the main character, is throwing for his friend, Harold. Michael, a successful lawyer living on the East Side, doesn't wear his homosexuality on his sleeve, so to speak, and he doesn't flaunt it either.

Several hours before the arrival of his guests, all of whom are gay of course, Michael receives a phone call from his old college roommate, Alan, who happens to be in town. Alan, of course, is straight. Alan, who apparently has no idea of his former roommate's sexual orientation, asks if he can come over for a visit. An alarmed Michael fends off Alan by telling him that he is having "some friends over." Of course, Michael neglects to tell Alan his friends, who include at least one very flamboyant character, an interior designer by the name of Emory, are…you know, well, gay.

Alan, still in blissful ignorance, responds by saying that the shindig sounds like fun. Michael, panicking at the prospect of his old classmate, who knew him before he started "playing for the other team" (as they used to say in those days), discovering his "secret," tries to discourage Alan from coming over, whereupon Alan breaks down and confesses that he is having trouble with his marriage and desperately needs to talk. Michael relents, and reluctantly informs his friends of the unsuspecting straight interloper's imminent arrival.

The other guests, already well into their cups, react with a collective "Oh well." Emory, the most flamboyant of the bunch—as well as the one who adheres most closely to the stereotypical image most Americans—myself included--had of gays in 1968, when the play debuted, "rehearses" for Alan's arrival by assuming his best "he man" persona and asking aloud, "So do you think the Giants are going to win the pennant this year?"

The stage is set for a most interesting party. When Alan arrives, he is shocked to find himself face-to-face with a four-man ass-grabbing line of male choristers led by Emory, tricked out in his best Fire Island uniform of polo shirt and tennis shoes, hoofing it up to the amplified sounds of *Heat Wave*.

Things sort of go south from there. Before the evening is over, more—many more—drinks and secrets are spilled, a few punches are thrown (by Alan at Emory), not a few tears are spilled, and Alan has his first up-close view of "homosexual" culture, as presumably does most of the audience.

And guess what? It turns out that "homosexuals"—even "fairies" like Emory—as well as homosexual couples, like the ones portrayed in *Boys*, are, except for their concern about their acceptance in general society (something which virtually all gays were paranoid about in those days, when the great preponderance of gays were still very much in the closet) not all that different than their counterparts in the heterosexual world, with many of the same issues, anxieties, and concerns.

Not a very revolutionary message, to be sure, but at a time when the vast majority of straight people had never met nor knew anyone who was openly gay and tended to deride homosexuals as "fags" and "queers"—an image (and self-image) that was reinforced by the rare gay or even rarer gay couple who turned up on the TV, it was groundbreaking.

The gay community itself—insofar as it was a community at that time—had very mixed feelings about *The Boys*. On the one hand, gays welcomed what was in fact the first portrayal of their world—albeit a rather skewed representation of their world—on the stage, or the screen. Others, like gay playwright Edward Albee, felt that this was negated by the excessive amount of self-laceration on display, which reinforced the general assumption amongst straights that gay people could not be happy, a message that ran directly counter to the new Gay Pride movement, which had exploded with full force the previous summer, the summer of 1969, during the so-called Stonewall riots.

Personally, I remember reading about the original play and the furor it created when it first came out in April, 1968, and was vaguely aware that it had since also been made into a movie, however I can't say that I was in a rush to see it when the film version, directed by William Friedkin—the same William Friedkin who would soon become famous for directing *The French Connection*—finally hit the theaters during the summer of 1970. At that time, I had given little thought to the homosexual lifestyle, and while I had seen some avant-garde films on my occasional forays to Manhattan, *The Boys in the Band* was off the grid for me.

However, as it happened, *Boys*, which was also one of the hit movies that turbulent summer, is what was on offer at the Parsons Theater, and, sure enough, as ushers are wont, I wound up seeing it, again and again. I think I wound up seeing *Boys* fifty times in all.

I also wound up liking it. Not so much for its "message," which didn't mean very much either way to me, but as a movie, or rather as a play: the movie was adapted directly from the play; also, somewhat unusually, it employed exactly the same cast.

The fact of the matter was that *Boys* was a very well-made play, with (for the most part) believable, empathetic characters and a compelling plot. (Even Edward Albee, who loathed it, admitted as such, calling it "a highly skillful play which I detested"). It also had crackling dialogue, all of which, or most of which, I wound up committing to memory, something else that happens when you see a movie fifty or sixty times. It wasn't long before I was completing the actors' lines for them as I ushered people to their seats.

And what lines they were. However you felt about gays, how could you not be captivated by an opening monologue like this (from Harold's belated arrival at his own birthday party):

What I am, Michael, is a thirty-two-year-old ugly, pockmarked Jew fairy, and if it takes a little while to pull myself together, and if I smoke a little pot before I get up the nerve to show my face to the world, it's nobody's goddamned business but my own. And how are you this evening?

I even found myself having errant thoughts, as I admired the action on-screen from the back of the theater, of giving acting a whirl someday myself. In addition to being an enticing creative outlet, it also held promise as a new way of looking at the world.

But it was just a summertime notion, and not something that I gave much conscious thought. I am sure that many other movie ushers over the years have had similar thoughts. For the moment, I was just happy to be home again with my parents and to give them the support they needed.

Of course I was also aware of some of the disturbing events taking place in the "real world," including the escalating civil war over the expanding war in Vietnam, which had reached a bloody apotheosis several months before when four college students were killed by Ohio National Guardsmen at Kent State University. After all, my minor was history, but ultimately my world was still a fairly parochial one as it was for many if not most of my peers, although now this remarkable film about a world and a lifestyle about which I knew little had opened my eyes a bit more.

****

THEN, the following September, after I had returned to Bridgeport to start my sophomore year, and while I was still brooding over my disappointment at not having made the varsity team, an odd thing happened: I noticed a poster affixed to a pillar in the lobby of North Hall announcing an audition for the well-regarded university theater's forthcoming production of…what was this?—*The Boys in the Band!*

Mind, if the audition had been for any other play I would have passed by it and not given it a second thought, but this was *The Boys in the Band!* The same play-cum-screenplay I had just seen over and over from the back of the Parsons Theater, and whose dialogue was virtually imprinted on my brain.

"Why not?" After all, what did I have to lose?

And so several nights later I eagerly reported to the green room of the Little Theater for a very different sort of tryout than I was used to, a tryout for the theatrical varsity, so to speak—for that is precisely what the university theater department, with its highly polished, well-attended productions, had grown into at the arts-friendly Bridgeport campus.

I was ambitious: I thought that I would try out for the part of Michael, the lead. *Imagine that!*

However, my hopes of making the cut were quickly dampened when I realized that the theater department was more like a club in the exclusive sense of the word and that virtually all of the other dozen or so students who had showed up knew each other. And that most of the main roles had already been cast and that the very jaded-looking Simon Cowell-like director who was nominally in charge of the exercise was simply going through the motions.

I was at the point of leaving when the student director, Ken Wolsk, realized that one of his pre-chosen cast was, for one reason or the other, not on the premises. *Imagine that!*

At the same moment his eyes fell on me. Perhaps, he asked in an audibly skeptical tone of voice, I might wish to take a shot at the role…

And which role was that? Not Michael, or Alan, or any of the other relatively non-flamboyant members of the closeted Band to whom I *might* have borne a passing resemblance (I stress *might*), but the *most* flamboyant one, Emory, he of the dainty white tennis shoes and swish manners!

"Emory?" I gulped.

"Yes, Emory," the director replied with a yawn.

74

Emory?! EMORY?! No way, I said to myself.

Wait, wait, another voice said… *Why not!*

Why not indeed. Whereupon I duly took the script and began reading the parts for Emory for the director while the other student thespians distractedly looked on.

I am not sure exactly what took hold of me—my competitive spirit, perhaps, as well as my relish for proving people *wrong.* In any case, just as Susan Boyle, the oafish Scottish singer who wound up wowing Simon Cowell and his fellow *Britain's Got Talent* judges at her now-celebrated 2008 televised audition, so did I that long-ago day in the green room of The Little Theater with my dead-on impression of Emory.

It was cool watching the expressions of the student jury rapidly morph from blasé to surprised, to impressed, to bowled over as I convincingly pranced and limp-wristed my way through Emory's lines, with nary a look at the script.

Of course, what the impressed director and his friends didn't know was that I already knew virtually all of the dialogue, including Emory's, by heart.

Regurgitating dialogue is one thing. But giving a credible, compassionate, not too OTT performance of a flaming queen—for *me*—good old straight and narrow Jesse Braverman, that was something else.

And so I did. Not only did I surprise the jaded director of the UB theatrical club and his buddies—I surprised myself. I *nailed* it! The moment the audition was over I knew from the assembled student thespians' expressions that I had the part.

And so I did. When I walked out of The Little Theater, having shed my Emory-ish expressions, I had a broad grin on my face.

****

However, my joy at being cast gave way to apprehension. Suddenly, I realized, a few months from then—it was now October and the production was scheduled for February—I would have to take the stage of the UB Student Center before hundreds of skeptical, if not openly leering undergraduates,

75

including, and especially my fellow "jocks," and do justice to this (to say the least) out-of-character role without making a laughingstock of myself. Tall bill.

Please bear in mind that before I had had absolutely no previous acting experience whatsoever. I HAD never even *wanted* to act.

And now I really had to *act*—no less act the part of a flaming *queen*! Talk about a spicy meatball.

Fortunately, once again, I *did* have expert help in the person of the department's accomplished and erudite acting coach, Franklin Lindsay, who took me under his wing. The fact that, in addition to being a brilliant and empathetic teacher, Lindsay, the senior and most-respected member of the Theatre Department was an experienced actor himself certainly added to his effectiveness as my dramaturgical "pitching coach."

Under Lindsay's tutelage I learned that if I wanted to "win the game" as Emory, I would have to give a *complete* performance— that everything I did, *every* line I declaimed, every gesture had to count, if I wanted to connect with the audience. He urged me to make Emory's actions speak even more loudly than his dialogue. Emory—my Emory, the one I was creating—had to provoke audience reaction with every gesture, and every movement.

Within a month or two, as I rehearsed the play with the other members of my new "Band," I found myself undergoing a remarkable transformation: I was not only *acting* the part of Emory, I was *becoming* Emory. I suppose you could call it The Method, although the decidedly unpretentious Lindsay never labeled his particular dramaturgical philosophy as such. In any case, I was getting it done.

In the meantime, I discovered that the character I had not wanted to read for at the original audition was, in fact, an actor's delight. Thanks to Professor Lindsay, as well as my own steadily rising self-confidence, I discovered that once I locked into the character and learned to stay in character, the basic challenge was a matter of listening to and playing the moment. I also saw what I had previously only intuited: that, for all his *bizarre* behavior, the role of Emory provided a vital link in conveying the basic message of the play (insofar as it had a message), i.e., that *all* God's creatures, even flaming queens, are essentially alike all over.

I also overcame my initial trepidation about how my outlandish new role affected my general "image" on campus, as well how my self-consciously masculine teammates on the JV baseball team perceived me. The rehearsals were challenging and enjoyable and I never confused the character I was portraying with my own identity, and if someone else did, that was their problem.

I found that I enjoyed moving back and forth between the two very different, if not diametrically opposed worlds of the dressing room and the locker room. I also found that, despite their overt differences, perhaps the theatre world and the jock world weren't as far apart as one might think. Was there really such a difference between the acting out of my fellow cast members, one or more of whom, for all I knew, might have actually been gay themselves, although no one actually came out and said so (although coming out, especially on a conservative campus like Bridgeport in 1971 would have required a particular act of bravado) and the swagger of the baseball guys? I think not.

And thus, in this most quixotic and unpredictable way—via a new outlet I had literally stumbled across—my consciousness, to use another word much in vogue back then, expanded. Super straight Jesse Braverman, the Emeralds and Jamaica High School pitcher, was *greening*. As well as seeing that perhaps there was a world beyond baseball, after all.

****

IN THE MEANTIME, I still had a performance to give.

Fast forward to February 1971, opening night. Thanks to the positive advance word from the few students who had seen us in rehearsals, as well as perhaps the notoriety of the subject matter, virtually all of the five-hundred-some odd seats in the UB Student Center were taken as far as I could see when I peeked from behind the curtain.

Two of the seats, I also knew, were taken by my parents, who had driven up from New York to see me perform, although I tried not to think about that.

And a minute later, with nary a moment's hesitation, out pranced Jesse Braverman—yes, *that* Jesse Braverman in his most campy, Emoryish manner, bearing a luscious casserole he had putatively baked for the occasion (actually the handiwork of a gifted stagehand).

I could almost hear my junior varsity teammates' collective gasp as I declaimed in my best mock-jock voice:

"So, do you think the Giants are going to win the pennant this year?!"

Cue nervous laughter…

Soon enough, though, as the tragic-comic arc of the play continued, and I continued to declaim my lines—while getting into a very authentic-looking confrontation with the student playing Alan, fisticuffs and all—the laughter died down, and with it perhaps some of that nervousness too, as the very real, and perhaps not *so* funny world of the "typical" gay person of that unliberated day was exposed on the stage of the University of Bridgeport Student Center, and people realized that they were watching a really great *play.*

Personally I was too caught up with my inaugural appearance on the stage to pay attention, but I could sense—in the same way that I could sense the attention of the crowd at one of my ball games—that the five hundred or so playgoers were riveted. Frankly I was more concerned with flubbing my lines. After all, this *was* my first time on the stage!

I could also sense the members of the audience's collective shock as they took in some of Crowley's more outrageous lines, including and especially the ones Alan heaves in my direction during our firefight:

Faggot! Fairy! Pansy! Queer! Cocksucker!
I'll kill you you goddam mincing swish!!!

And so on.

Withal, fairly incendiary stuff for 1971.

And then, in a blink, it seems, all of the *Band* members were on the stage after the curtain had fallen, taking our bows to thunderous applause. It sure *sounded* as if we had hit a home run. The review in the next day's *Scribe*, the Bridgeport paper, confirmed it, lauding our polished student production for successfully depicting "the lack of understanding homosexuals receive"—remember this was 1971—while singling out my "sparkling" performance, by way of presenting "a credible rendition of the status quo [sic] homosexual." (Again, remember that this *was* 1971.)

Fran Bacon, the no-nonsense, butch-cut varsity baseball coach, who, it turned out, had been in attendance that epochal midwinter evening, along with some of the other wide-eyed members of the Purple Knights, certainly found my turn as Emory memorable.

"Braverman," he remarked to me, unjestingly, the next time I saw him during pre-season training, "If we ever go on the road you can have a room to yourself!"

That may have been the most gratifying notice of them all.

Much to my delight, Harry and Midge, after getting over their astonishment at my new outlet, no less my choice of role, thoroughly enjoyed the opening night performance. Somehow, I could distinguish my mother's uproarious laughter among the packed house. And to think, less than three years before, I had visited her at Creedmoor.

If I needed evidence that she was on the road to recovery, her familiar pealing laughter supplied it.

Life is strange. And all because I had happened to get a job as an usher at the Parsons Theatre while *The Boys in the Band* was in the middle of its run.

****

ALTHOUGH it probably would be an exaggeration to say that I was stagestruck, I was now sufficiently fascinated with the theatre, as well as admiring of Professor Lindsay, whose directions had been so crucial to my successfully understanding and conveying the character of Emory, that the following term I decided to take an acting course with my distinguished acting

79

tutor. I also was curious to see whether I was a one-trick pony and could be as successful with another acting role without having first seen it performed fifty times, as I had with Emory and *The Boys*.

My doubts on that score were dispelled when, again with Lindsay's encouragement and assistance, I nailed a very different role, that of Lomov in the classic Checkhov play, *The Proposal*. So perhaps this thespian thing wasn't such a fluke, after all.

Did I harbor any illusions about conquering The Great White Way? Not quite. Although I had, much to my surprise, proven that I had a flair for acting, I wasn't sufficiently deluded, nor did Lindsay encourage me to think, that there was any rational possibility of my becoming a successful full-time professional actor. I liked the stage—actually I *loved* it. However, although I felt sure that I wanted to continue to make the theater part of my life, that was still a far cry from thinking that I had a vocation for it. Additionally, the practical, "candy store" side of me bridled at the thought of actually trying to make a living as an actor, even if I could.

What *was* my vocation? What *was* my place outside of the cozy bubble of college, in the great unknown we undergraduates of the day liked to call The Real World?

I still had some pondering to do on that score. But in the meantime, I certainly had broadened my horizons, hadn't I? And ultimately isn't that what going to college is supposed to be about?

In later years, including recent ones, I would return to the theatre world, both as a source of fun, as well as solace. I had indeed found a new love, an alternate one you might say.

Life is strange. And wonderful. And so it certainly seemed in 1971 and 1972, as I made my eye-opening, mind-expanding way across the diverse playing fields of the University of Bridgeport.

****

MEANWHILE, a number of other copacetic things happened while I was at college to further expand my horizons.

80

Thus, one evening, while I was meandering through the basement of my dorm, North Hall, I happened to notice a ferocious ping-pong game going on between one of my dorm mates, a burly undergrad, and a member of the football squad, and a diminutive Asian man.

The latter contestant, who turned out to be an engineering professor of Japanese extraction named Seichi Takeiuchi (I am quite positive that I misspelled that) who possessed a lightning backhand, was winning. After the heaving and panting football player went down in flames, I stepped up and offered to take his place. I might not be Forest Gump, but I remembered something about the game from the games I had played with my brother on the ping-pong table in our basement.

Anyway, I was always game for a worthy contest.

So up I stepped, and off we went, whacking and whirling away before a bemused group of berobed North Hallers—those were also the days before co-ed housing (did I say *co-eds?*). Inevitably perhaps, I also went down to defeat before my fierce, if soft-spoken opponent, although not before giving The Honorable Professor T. a good game—good enough for him to invite me to a rematch the following night in the basement recreation room of his off-campus apartment building.

Thus began what turned out to be a new weekly activity that would last for the remainder of my years at Bridgeport. Although I don't recall us saying much to each other, I was nevertheless charmed and flattered that a member of the faculty, and particularly an Asian or Asian American, would engage me in this manner. Mind, this was at a time when Asian Americans, particularly Japanese Americans, were still dealing with the vestigial residue of prejudices against *them* remaining from World War II.

And so, via the quixotic vehicle of ping-pong, my "coming of consciousness," progressed.

||*|*

81

AT THE SAME TIME, my field of vision was further broadened by some of the books I was reading in and out of class and the lyrics of the music I was listening to.

You know how when you were young and you happened to come across a book, whether it be a philosophical tract or a novel that seemed to reinforce and validate the things you were thinking about? One such book that a lot of my peers seemed to be reading during their off hours was *Jonathan Livingston Seagull*.

Another book, which had a profound impression on many of my peers as well as myself, was *The Greening of America*, the tribute to the emerging counterculture by self-styled prophet-futurist Charles Reich. Originally published as an article in *The New Yorker*, *The Greening*'s slightly spacey but still cogent thesis was that there were three types of consciousness in the world: Consciousness I, which corresponded to the world-view of rural farmers and small business people, and which was principally the legacy of nineteenth-century America; Consciousness II, which represented the increasingly outdated and obsolete, consumer-based world-view and cultural climate of postwar America, and our parents' more practical-minded generation; and Consciousness III, the ecologically-influenced world view of the counter-culturally-oriented 60s generation.

Reich's bestselling book, which I read for a philosophy class I took during my junior year with Professor Edward D'Angelo, mixed sociological analysis with encomia to rock music, cannabis, and blue jeans, arguing that taken together these phenomena and artifacts embodied a fundamental, permanent revolution in world-view, a tenet I was somewhat skeptical of.

In the end, as we know, that Great Revolution was less permanent, or perhaps I should say more superficial, than either Reich or some of his more enthusiastic adherents foresaw, as two of the above countercultural artifacts, i.e., rock music and blue jeans, were quickly "co-opted" (another word much in favor then) by mainstream American culture, while Reich's "Consciousness III" left considerably less of an imprint than either he or some of his most fervent adherents predicted, while marijuana and the other drugs that were supposed to help perpetuate that "higher state" simply became a means of getting high.

What I took from Reich was the idea—you might call it a corollary of Consciousness III—that the best way of changing the world was to lead a life that reflected and embodied one's own world-view, which in my case was comprised, or came to be comprised of, equal parts commitment, civility, and tolerance, leavened with a bit of humor—sort of a combination of my parents' and Joe Austin's hardworking, no-nonsense ethos with a generous amount of the "you can be all you want to be" feeling of the 60s set.

Rock music? Fine—although personally I preferred Simon and Garfunkel and Bob Dylan. Blue jeans? Sure.

Marijuana? No thanks!

In the meantime I also learned a little bit more about the art of critical thinking from Edward D'Angelo, one of the several teachers who helped further open my eyes during my sojourn at Bridgeport, and who also helped solidify my notion of someday becoming a teacher myself.

****

SPEAKING of pot, as much as I sympathized with aspects of Charles Reich's New World Order, I was permanently disabused of the notion of experimenting with that or any of the other mind-expanding substances which he advocated, when, at the start of my junior year at Bridgeport, I had the memorable, and considerably frightening experience of "hosting"—if that is the word—my old childhood mentor and surrogate older brother, Bruce Lerro, while he was passing—or should I say tripping--through the Connecticut area.

By tripping, I mean literally. If my beliefs and lifestyle had been mildly affected by the strange, exciting, and confusing times we were passing through, my hypersensitive, intellectual friend had caught them full force. Intrigued with the Haight-Ashbury lifestyle, unhappy with the strictures of middle-class Jamaica life,

83

my old neighbor had become a full-fledged Flower Power person, a.k.a. a hippie.

Now, in the fall of 1972, the same year that would see the political greening of America reach its apogee with the nomination of George McGovern as Democratic candidate for President and the end of the High Counterculture years, Bruce was on his way to join a cool commune he had heard about that was located in the Boston area when he called me at Bridgeport.

Unfortunately *he* didn't sound so cool. In fact, Bruce sounded very out of it. The reason? He had dropped some bad acid, as they used to say. Or maybe he had dropped some good acid (if there is such a thing), but he had taken too much of it. Anyway, he didn't make much sense. All he knew was that he needed some help.

He certainly did. The next thing I knew I was driving my incoherent friend to the emergency room of Bridgeport Hospital so he could "come down" from his freakout. If the Revolution had a dark side, this was it: sitting in the waiting room of an emergency room while one's tripped-out friend was lying on a table in the next room being sedated.

Fortunately, Bruce recovered from his trip, although it took him a while to shake off his dalliance with the counterculture. Today he teaches psychology in California and is a published author.

For my part, the most consciousness-expanding substances I ever "dropped" or were interested in during my own college days were books and ideas. *Was* today the first day of the rest of my life? Absolutely.

In the meantime, I decided, I had better finish my degree. Ultimately, you could take the practical-minded boy who had helped his parents count the pennies out of the candy store, but you couldn't take the candy store out of the boy.

CHAPTER 5:
THE RIGHT FIELD AT THE RIGHT TIME

Jesse Braverman has the essential teaching capacity that cannot be learned. He is keenly interested in young people and in teaching them. He conducts a classroom discussion with vigor and imagination. The students respond to him. He is aware of the need to be fair and the students value him for it. He has a sense of humor which enables him to weather difficulty.

  —from my first teacher evaluation, from Charles Burwell, the
    chairman of the Social Studies department at Darien High
    School, Darien, Connecticut, November, 1972.

It would be remiss of me to speak of Jack's education and not mention Mr. Braverman, for he has done for Jack what few individuals have done. He's made people stop and take the time to see what this little guy has to offer. He's also helped Jack to increase his level of confidence.

  —from a letter by the mother of one of my special needs
    students, 1975.

THE CONTOURS of my future existence in the Real World had become much clearer by the spring of my senior year at college as a result of two significant developments.

For one, I had made a tentative decision about what I would do once I got Out There. I decided that I would enter the promising field of special education. Hopefully, I would be able to combine a career in special ed, as that promising field was

85

called, with a position coaching baseball at some point. That was the plan, at least.

Although I was originally leaning toward teaching social studies, there were few positions available in that field at the time, so special ed seemed the more pragmatic choice. Perhaps inspired by my experience with Joey Rappapoort, I was also drawn by the challenge of working with students who had potential but had challenges to overcome. I also found it exciting to enter a field that was still in its embryonic stage. At any rate, I had made my Decision and both of my advisors at college, as well as my parents, had agreed that it was a sound one, as it indeed turned out to be.

Additionally, a woman had come into my life. Her name was Anna Sipp. I met Anna during the spring of 1972 during an atypical sortie to a nightclub in Mineola, Long Island, while I was home for spring break. After I and the attractive young woman I found myself talking to, or trying to talk to, had gotten through our initial "Whats,?!" we discovered, to our mutual delight, that we had a considerable amount in common. For one, both of us were interested in becoming teachers. After a few more "Whats?," I gathered that Anna was interested in becoming an art therapist and was attending Suffolk Community College.

Frankly, I was just looking to talk to someone. I wasn't necessarily looking to get married. I hadn't even had a proper girlfriend yet.

And yet, as occurred during those innocent, pre-romantic due diligence days, that—after several promising dates including one sleep over that confirmed that we were physically compatible—is what happened. Before you knew it, I had it all worked out. First, we were going to get married. The fact that Anna and I were twenty and twenty-one years of age, respectively, and that we had never spent more than a weekend together nor shared a home didn't enter into the beguiling Venus Paradise drawing I had sketched of Anna and my future.

Fortunately, my parents approved of Anna, and her parents did of me (not that either had much choice in the matter): done deal. The only thing that still had to be worked out was where we would live and study after each of us had graduated. By the fall of my senior year, all of our plans were set. By this time, Anna had transferred to the State University of New York in Buffalo, and I had applied for admission to the graduate program in special education at the State University of New York in Albany, which was known to have one of the best programs in special education in the northeast.

Of course there was the small matter of getting in, however with the 3.6 grade point average I had managed to achieve, and top references to boot, I didn't think that that would be a problem. Anna and I were going to get married, I was going to get my master's in special ed at the State University of New York at Albany, Anna would get her degree in art therapy, and together—me the special ed teacher extraordinaire, while acting on the side, and she the art therapist—would morph into a larger therapeutic entity and help green the educational world. And we would, of course, live happily ever after.

That, at least, was the plan.

Once in a while when I passed through the TV room of my dorm that term, I noticed that something called the Watergate affair about some dirty tricks the incumbent president had played during the previous campaign, or rather the president's men had played, was increasingly occupying the attention of the country, as well as a good number of my peers. Of course this was concerning, but my focus was now squarely on my and Anna's future, just like the nice Jewish boy from Queens I still was.

In the end, I had quit moaning about my "lost" baseball career, and had cut down on the ping-pong and hit the books at Bridgeport. Having a serious girlfriend, no less one who I was planning on marrying as soon as I had tossed my graduation cap, doubtlessly had helped me settle down. Put simply, I had grown up. I even wound up graduating magna cum laude, to my parents' surprise and delight (as well as mine).

There was just the small matter of getting into SUNY Albany.

****

IT turns out that this wasn't such a small matter. Indeed, I learned, only fourteen out of eighty applicants who applied each year to the prestigious program were accepted. The key factor in determining admission was an all-day on-site interview with the SUNY special education faculty. Said interview was scheduled for April.

I was understandably nervous when I boarded the bus for an all-day journey from Bridgeport to Albany where I and a contingent of a dozen candidates were put through the paces. Yes, the odds were against me, I told myself as I arrived, but I was determined to make it: my future, our future, depended on it. To put it in baseball terms, I had to throw three strikes.

And so I did. First, there was a written test. Passed that. Strike one. Next, we were shown a series of video vignettes depicting hypothetical classroom situations. Then the camera would be turned off and each of us were asked how we would handle the situation we had just seen. I was fairly confident that I had passed that one. Strike two. So far so good.

The final test, however, was a killer, though: each of us, we were informed, would be videotaped teaching a lesson to a "student." The goal of the lesson, we were told, was to teach an abstract concept to an individual with limited background knowledge. Specifically, we would be preparing a recent Hispanic immigrant for his citizenship test by inculcating him in the principle of checks and balances enshrined in the U.S. Constitution.

First we were handed a synopsis of the Constitution, including an explanation of the checks and balances principle, with a view toward developing a coherent lesson for student X, a swarthy-complexioned young man who soon sat down opposite me on the other side of a one-way window. Said fellow could not see me, but I could see him; theoretically this would enhance the "objectivity" of the test.

In the event, I was so busy preparing my lesson for "X" that I missed out on the note in the instructions informing me that "X" was himself a SUNY graduate student who would be role-playing the part of a Dominican who had recently arrived on the mainland with limited skills.

I actually thought the dark-complexioned young man in front of me was about to take his citizenship test in his pursuit of the American Dream. *Imagine that!*

Consequently, I labored over the preparation of my lesson plan utterly oblivious to the true identity of the earnest-seeming fellow seated opposite me, while my board of examiners looked on from behind a one-way window. The other applicants—presumably—had read the instructions and knew what was what. But for me this was the real thing. One would think that this would have been a disadvantage, but in fact it wasn't—although it certainly made me jittery!

After somewhat nervously exchanging introductions with "Jose" as a video camera mercilessly recorded our meeting, I had a brief conversation with him in order to learn more about him, as well as to gauge his facility with language. It appeared that "Jose's" English was adequate for the questions regarding the constitutional checks and balances I had prepared. Little did I realize that English was his *only* language!

I began the lesson by asking "Jose" whether it was possible for the president to make a mistake. After some studied hesitation—my interviewee was a fairly good actor himself, it turned out (although he himself didn't realize that I thought he was for real)—"Jose" admitted that yes, it was possible for the U.S. president to make a mistake, and I explained how and why the founding fathers had embedded a system of checks and balances in the Constitution for that very reason. We then went on to discuss the related concept of the separation of powers.

And so on and so forth. Now things got to be sticky, as "Jose" began casting puzzled looks in my direction, and began "acting" confused and pretended to have difficulty understanding my explanations.

I realized that I was in a spot. I began to sweat. The "game,'" i.e., my acceptance into SUNY Albany, I knew, was hanging on what I did next.

So I scrambled. Fortunately, I had taken Spanish as my required language course at Jamaica High. I hadn't actually conducted a conversation in Spanish since then, but, oh well, here we go…

Switching to Spanish, I haltingly explained the concept of separation of powers to "Jose" as best as I could, while my unseen "jury" looked on from behind the one-way mirror. "Jose" smiled and nodded: he was indeed a good actor. However he didn't say very much. That was OK as long as he got it.

Little did I suspect that the reason why "Jose" didn't say very much was because he didn't speak Spanish!

Imagine that.

In any case, as I later learned, my genuine ignorance of my interlocutor's equally genuine ignorance of Spanish worked to my advantage by allowing me to display my resourcefulness under pressure, a knack that would, and continues to serve me well.

Of course, I didn't know that at the time. I thought I had thrown it down the middle, but I couldn't be sure. What *were* those guys on the other side of the one-way glass really thinking as I struggled to make myself clear to "Jose?" Who knew? All I knew is that I had given it my best shot. As the saying goes, do your duty and leave the rest to the gods.

In any case, it wouldn't be very long before I found out.

Several nail-biting weeks later, I opened my tiny mailbox at my Bridgeport dorm and beheld the anxiously-awaited envelope with the SUNY seal. My heart was pounding in my ear as I tore the Damoclean missive open.

And there, to my heart-palpitating delight, in the second paragraph, were the words I was longing to read:

"We are pleased to offer you admission into the graduate program of special education…"

Deliverance. Now I could fill in that section of my Venus Paradise drawing of Anna and my happily-ever-after future.

****

90

THE next few months were a happy blur. Two months later, as my parents proudly watched on, there I was, moving the tassel on my mortarboard from left to right at the graduation ceremony for the Bridgeport class of 1973. My parents were even more thrilled when they looked down at the embossed program to see that their son had graduated magna cum laude. Imagine that!

Resilient man that he was, my father had rebounded from the loss of the candy store, and, at the age of sixty, had managed to find a steady clerical position with Bear Stearns, the stock brokerage, while taking courses at night to continue his education.

My mother, Midge, was also doing somewhat better. The year before, unfortunately, she had been hospitalized again, but fortunately this time my father had had the good sense to take her to St. Vincent's Hospital in Manhattan, where she was diagnosed with hyperthyroidism for which she received proper medication, which helped her enormously. For the moment, all was well with the Bravermans.

Two months later, in August, there my parents were again, wearing their Saturday best, along with their best smiles—mixed with perhaps a slight trace of astonishment—as I got married to Anna at a large, festive, and ecumenical wedding at the Fox Hollow Inn, in Woodbury, New York. Although we thought about inviting Joe, we ultimately decided not to. Weddings were just not Joe's thing. However, he was there in spirit.

And then the next thing we knew there we were, the two lovebirds, happily ensconced in a pleasant apartment in Albany where Anna made me breakfast every day before I sailed off to class at SUNY, and, after a big matching kiss and hug, she flew off to Troy to continue her studies at Russell Sage. Looking good!

First, of course, I had to nail that degree. No problem.

****

TO be sure, the year I spent at SUNY Albany was a heady and eye-opening—if occasionally confusing—one. I enjoyed my courses immensely, even if some of them were a bit theoretical for me. It quickly became clear to me that I had chosen the right field at the right time: there was little doubt that I would find gainful employment in this rapidly expanding discipline.

At the same time, I realized that ultimately I would have to sort out a lot on my own.

The courses I took and the feedback I received from my teachers soon confirmed that special education was a good intellectual fit for me, even if I found some of the more "experimental" material I had to imbibe somewhat hard to chew. Somewhat to my surprise, it turned out, I had a flair for pedagogy.

However, and fortunately, despite the speculative leanings of some of the more abstract teachers, and unlike some other special education programs, SUNY Albany was definitely not in the business of turning out pedagogues.

Indeed, the premise of the program, as with all sound teacher education programs, was that the best way to turn out an effective special education teacher was by letting him or her do the real thing. Reading books about theory was all very well and good, but the vital thing was getting in there and mixing it up with real students in as many different settings as possible.

The theory, really, was optional—unless of course I intended to become an academic myself, which I certainly did not. Besides, it was the contention of the professor whom I admired the most, Frank Vellutino, that the most important requirement for a special education teacher was, as I suspected, a large store of common sense, along with a bottomless well of compassion.

The core of the program comprised two back-to-back internships, first a semester teaching severely disabled students in an alternate, or segregated setting—to use the pejorative that used to be attached to this type of setting in the "bad old days," i.e., the days before special education was recognized as a discrete and fundamental specialty in its own right and learning disabled and otherwise handicapped students were treated with the dignity and respect they deserved.

This part of my training, I learned, would take place at the SUNY downtown campus at the Stage School, a program for elementary school students who had been excluded from the

Albany public school system because they were either severely physically or psychologically disabled. That was where I would be based in the fall.

For the spring semester, I was set to do my thing, so to speak, in a public school, Hillside Elementary School, in the Schenectady suburb of Niskayuna, where I would have the responsibility of supporting students with special needs who were being integrated into the regular curriculum as the new, if still somewhat controversial received wisdom in the field, prescribed, while also remediating these students' basic skill sets.

The theoretical component of the SUNY program was less important than the practical aspect. In any event, by the end of the year I would, presumably, feel more confident about my career choice as well as my hunch that I indeed had something special to contribute to it—as well as in which sort of setting, and with which type of special needs student, I would be happiest and most effective making that contribution.

That was the idea. It certainly would be interesting to see. And who knows? Perhaps by the time I actually received my degree I would have developed a rudimentary educational philosophy of my own from mixing what I incorporated from my classroom work (or chose *not* to incorporate) with what I learned in the Real World of special needs.

And so off with my notebooks and good intentions I went, along with a bag sandwich supplied by my up-and-coming art therapist wife! Obviously, I was at one of the great crossroads of my life, and it felt good, almost like starting a doubleheader after two weeks of rest.

****

TO BE SURE, as quickly became evident, the field I was entering, special education, a phrase which actually was only then coming into practice, was itself at quite a historic, as well as a philosophical—not to mention a legal—crossroads.

I well-remembered from my own fleeting encounter with special-needs students when I was in elementary school the

93

stigma attached to the handicapped or "the retarded" as they were termed in the "bad old days" of the 1960s. Indeed, it seems that the "bad old days" were just coming to an end when I had the good fortune to enter the field, thanks to the passage of a recent landmark piece of legislation, the 1975 Individuals with Disabilities Act (IDEA).

Before we discuss the IDEA, perhaps a short discussion of the history of special education is in order.

It is well to note that education of the disabled didn't even exist, in the formal sense of the word, until the twentieth century. Both disabled children and adults were generally considered untouchables, a subspecies of human; legal mandates denied them their basic civil rights; theological canons excluded them from church membership; philosophers pronounced them incapable of mental or moral improvement.

Often times the disabled were confined in jails or almshouses without decent food or clothing. Unsurprisingly, in this pejorative, even penal environment, there was little interest in or support for educating them, no less any feeling that the public had any responsibility for doing so. The burden—as it was indeed generally seen—for educating the physically or mentally disabled, or "cripples" or "the insane," as they were referred to, or worse, fell upon the private sector.

In 1817 a number of prominent citizens of Hartford, Connecticut established an "asylum," as they called it, for the "deaf" and "dumb:" the fact that these two different types of special-needs students were lumped together speaks volumes about the primitive state of special education at this time. A number of private schools for the "feeble-minded," as they were also called during the nineteenth century, were also established.

However, the quality of schooling that was offered at such institutions continued to be backward, and in the case of the mentally disabled, even destructive, because of the received wisdom that mental retardation was a form of emotional disturbance, if not an outright curse.

Interestingly, it was a novelist, Charles Dickens, who first shed light on the shameful and reprehensible state of the handicapped in his novel, *Bleak House*. Although his harrowing tale essayed to describe and publicize the condition of the handicapped in England, the horrific picture the writer drew could have applied to both sides of the Atlantic.

Although some progress in ameliorating the treatment and education of the handicapped was made in the late nineteenth century and early twentieth century, the whole thrust was as much to keep the handicapped and disabled away from the rest of society as it was to succor and uplift them. The notion that one day these children could, should, or would be integrated into the mainstream of education, no less that they could become model citizens, was as remote as that of sending a man to the moon.

There was additional progress after World War II, as Civitas, an association of community service clubs, and parental advocacy groups like the unfortunately named National Association for Retarded Children and the Council for Exceptional Children, provided training for teachers of children with developmental disorders; however, the very names of the organizations underscored the fact that these children were still considered inferior.

Additionally, the 1954 Brown vs. Board of Education decision by the Supreme Court, guaranteeing equal educational opportunities for all students regardless of color, also helped improve matters by putting the issue of how to treat special-needs students in a favorable comparable context. If black students were being denied their basic rights by not being allowed the same educational opportunities as white students, as the Court ruled, then why should special-needs students also be discriminated against, as they clearly were.

Good point! Nevertheless, even as late as the 1960s, when I was in school, only about one out of five special-needs students could be said to be receiving anything approaching a good or adequate education, while many states explicitly discriminated against such students. Personally, the only contact I had had with a special-needs student before I became a special education teacher myself was with my friend Billy's schizophrenic brother,

Joey, and as much as I sympathized with him, as well as empathized with Bill, I can't say I ever wondered whether anyone was educating him, which was typical of the bias of the period.

The historic 1975 IDEA legislation enjoined schools to provide free appropriate public education to students with a wide range of disabilities, including physical handicaps, speech defects, vision and language problems, and other learning disorders, while also compelling school districts to provide such schooling in the least restrictive environment possible.

As a result of this vital and overdue legislation, tens of thousands of school-aged children were provided with some form of special education. For these students, the new legislation was just as significant—indeed special—as Brown vs. Board of Education, if not more so. At the same time, the bill, which became the legislative foundation for federal funding of special education, gave special education and special education teachers new pride and respect, while also increasing manifoldly the available opportunities in the field.

Put another way, special education, which had been somewhat in the shadows, was finally having its day in the sun. Although the landmark legislation was enacted after I completed my training, it was clear even then that the field was in a state of positive flux, and the newfound and welcome attention our previously neglected sector of education was suddenly receiving certainly put a spring in my and my fellow prospective teachers' heels.

First, of course, I had to finish my field training itself, which took place in two diametrically different settings and exposed me to two different forms of special education, while allowing me to narrow my own career choices and shape and elucidate my own philosophy of special education. The first setting was the Stage School, SUNY's on-site program for students who had been excluded from the Albany Public Schools for various reasons, including severe disability and neurological impairment. Most of the students at Stage were nonverbal.

Progress at the school was understandably slow, and instruction was primarily targeted at development of self-help skills and rudimentary educational concepts. Resistant behaviors ranged the gamut from passive resistance to aggressive acting out. Frankly, it wasn't the happiest time for me. I remember grumbling to myself that I didn't know that I would be earning my master's degree in a boys' bathroom teaching a recalcitrant child toileting skills.

I did manage to become close with a young boy, Jim. Jim had suffered serious brain damage after he had been hit by a car. Because he breathed through a tracheotomy, Jim unnerved me at first, but over the course of the term I grew accustomed to it, along with the apparatus he needed to keep his airway clear. As is generally the case with this sort of student, progress was agonizingly slow and painfully achieved. After several weeks of silence and little or no cooperation on his end, much to my delight, Jim. began to speak and perform some basic educational activities. He also seemed to become more comfortable with me, and started to show small, if undeniably measurable improvement.

Still, as pleased as I was by the little help I was able to bring this profoundly handicapped child, by the end of the term I was fairly confident that this type of special education was not for me. That said, I have tremendous admiration and respect for those teachers who work in the particularly challenging sector of special education. Once the semester was completed, my relationship with the school, as well as Jim, ceased. Sometimes I wonder what happened to Jim. I regret not ever finding out.

****

MY PUBLIC SCHOOL internship placement for the spring semester, at the Hillside Elementary School in Niskayuna, was all around a happier and more pleasant experience for me, as well as one that pointed me in the direction that my teaching career would ultimately go.

In contrast to the Stage School, where I worked with students on a one-to-one basis, my position at Niskayuna was that of Resource Room teacher, a somewhat nebulous role in which I had the dual responsibility of both supporting students with

97

special needs in the regular curriculum, while simultaneously remedying, or trying to remedy deficiencies or weaknesses in their basic skills.

At the same time, because special education was in a state of high flux, my job as Resource Room teacher at Niskayuna exposed me to the myriad educational approaches that were coming to the fore at the time, while also helping me decide which one worked best for me and *my* students, thereby allowing me to refine my own philosophy for teaching special ed. I must confess that many of these new-fangled and occasionally kooky (if well-intentioned) methods made little to no sense to me, insofar as they had little if any relevance to the educational weaknesses they were intended to correct or ameliorate.

Thus, for example, I failed to see the connection between helping students to improve their reading skills with having them walk on balance beams or navigate a quasi-Army-like basic training obstacle course, as some of the newly-minted "experts" in the suddenly "hot" field of special education recommended and my more impressionable young fellow novitiates were doing.

For my part, I preferred to have my students actually *read* or try to read, in a sedentary position rather than airborne, but that was just me. It may not sound terribly sophisticated, but I have always believed that a student needed to actually be engaged in reading in order to show progress with his reading!

It was also while I was at Niskayuna that I came to the "radical" conclusion that if one was going to "mainstream" students, i.e., integrate special need students with their "normal" peers—as one of the more sensible "new" theories that was achieving increasing acceptance at that time, and one that I enthusiastically endorsed, held—then their instructors ought to be mainstreamed, as well, i.e., encouraged to teach courses and/or initiate or participate in course-related or extracurricular activities involving the rest of the school, as well.

My preference, of course, would have been to have become involved in coaching baseball in some way, as I would eventually do at Bethlehem. Unfortunately, no such opportunity for "mainstreaming" myself, so to speak, availed itself during my short, "test run" at Niskayuna, though I did request and receive permission from the school principal, Ray Pressman, to direct a student play with a mixed cast of special needs students and regular education students, which turned out to be a very satisfying experience, and merited a round of applause from the student audience.

Fortunately, as much as I would like to think of myself as a pedagogical wizard, a number of other special education instructors and department chairmen across the country had a similar epiphany, and the notion of mainstreaming the special needs teacher *as well* as his or her students, is now considered common practice. As a result of this "double mainstreaming," when it is successfully practiced, Resource Room students who previously might have been invisible are no longer so, while the special ed teacher has a chance to interact with the entire student body, thus diminishing the stigma attached to special education.

At the same time, for it to work, mainstreaming also depends on the approval and cooperation of the rest of the teachers in the school, something which doesn't always happen, particularly in the absence of a dynamic and forward-minded principal. Fortunately, the head of Hillside was such an administrator.

All in all, except for a nine-day bout with the measles, which resulted in the longest ever sick leave I would ever take, up until the tragic derailment of the future and separate coaching career I would eventually grow at Bethlehem (more about that soon), my experience at Hillside was a happy and fulfilling one, serving both as a laboratory for me to try out and hone my own ideas about a sector of education that was just then coming into its own, while reconfirming that I had chosen the right field in which to make my career, and, hopefully, my mark.

In June the apprenticeship phase of my education formally came to an end when I received my master's in special education, along with my fellow future special education teachers-to-be from SUNY Albany, in an agreeable ceremony, which Anna attended, at the school's vast, futuristic campus.

Everything was still going according to plan.

Now I just needed to find a school where I could do my thing.

My mother Midge, aged 17, on the left, with two of her classmates from Marshall High School in Chicago around 1932.

A quarter of a century later, happily ensconced in Jamaica, Midge poses in her apron in front of our first candy store. Customers came for her radiant smile and my egg creams. Unfortunately the smile masked deeper problems.

My first day on a ball field at Edison Oval, in 1956, across the street from Jamaica High School, the same outdoor classroom where I learned about baseball and life from my mentor, Joe Austin. As you can see, I still had something to learn about baseball. Joe would soon fix that.

A snapshot of Joe and his kids, including my brother Roger and I, later that same year at Edison Oval. The boys are future Shannons and Emeralds. I'm center in the front row. Roger is behind my right shoulder. As you can see, I had no trouble fitting in.

Roger and I in front of the first Harry and Midge's Candy Store, around 1956. For the first years of my life that store, and a second one my parents would later open in Flushing, would be the center of my life and a source of much happiness, as well as heartbreak.

Two years later I was already an ace. Here I am practicing my
fastball at Bradley's Bar and Grill, next door.

My elementary school friends, the late Jimmy Gonedes, with
whom I concocted a famous—if notional—entomological
experiment, and my best friend, Billy Rappaport.

My wonderful, hard-working father, Harry, standing in front of the Flushing store, early one Sunday morning around 1965. Behind him are stacked the Sunday papers which were the store's bread and butter and which we all helped put together.

Harry and Midge, around 1966, holding hands. Two years later Midge would suffer a nervous breakdown for which she was hospitalized, traumatizing the family—and myself—in the process, but my father's devotion to her never wavered.

Here I am practicing my fastball for real as ace left-hander for the Beavers, the varsity baseball team of my high school, Jamaica High School, in 1968. The look on my face says it all. Baseball was everything to me.

THE SCRIBE

15¢ •Thursday Edition • Vol. 43 No. 33 • Feb. 25, 1971

UNIVERSITY OF BRIDGEPORT

Liberalized Liquor Proposal Offered

A proposal which would allow liquor in all dorms was presented to residence counselors during a Residence Hall Staff Meeting last month. The proposal was authored and presented by Howard Giles, director of residence halls.

Although specifics of the proposal were not revealed it was indicated that if the proposal was passed and agreed upon, there would, of course, be various restrictions imposed. Giles said that questions arose as to the distribution of liquor in specified areas of dorms. Should the allowance be limited to particular areas, such as just the rooms, or should it be allowed anywhere in the dorm, or, perhaps, even outside the dorms.

One of the main reasons for the consideration of the proposal is the favorable liquor activity report received from the new resi-

proposal made by Giles. Although Wolff initiated the review, he does have some reservations concerning the eventual outcome if the proposal is favorably recommended. He considers the situation rather complex, and he feels that if a very liberal liquor policy is accepted, there might possibly be requests for the use of marijuana on campus. "This is a rule and policy which raises close scrutiny," he said, "because there is some question as to whether it is really necessary and meaningful to the University community."

As the situation presently stands, the recommendation will again be presented at the next staff meeting, scheduled sometime this month. If approved, the proposal then must go to Dr. Wolff and University President Dr. Thurston E. Manning for final approval.

Scribe Photo—Mitchen

ROBERT LADANYI JOINS . . . Rollin Reese, Steven Finkel and Jesse Braverman in a little soft shoe in scene from "The Boys in the Band." The play, which deals with the plight of the misunderstood homosexual, goes into its final performance on campus tonight before going on the road.

Unable to play for the varsity at the University of Bridgeport, I found another surprising—and no less gratifying—outlet in the theater. My first role: Emory in the theater club's well-received 1971 adaptation of *The Boys in the Band*, as seen on the front page of the college newspaper, *The Scribe*.

105

I also found love—at least for a while—with my first wife, Anna. Here we are in a high spirited portrait shortly after we married in 1973. The high spirits were short-lived.

My boyhood friend Bruce Lerro and I checking out the diamond action at Geer Field, in South Troy, the home field of the La Salle Cadets, around 1975. Thirty years later I would become the Cadets' coach.

Enjoying the company of my special-needs students, and vice versa, as Resource Room teacher at Bethlehem Middle School in 1996. "Special ed" wasn't the first subject I wanted to teach, but it was the right subject for me.

My first entry to the world of coaching was via women's sports. Here I am huddling with the BCHS women's basketball team, the Lady Eagles, in 1988. I coached women's basketball for twenty-seven years.

I also coached women's soccer at Bethlehem for twenty-four years. Here I am with my girls in 1999. It's true: girls can do anything boys can!

In the meantime I was also fortunate to find lasting love with my second wife, Debbie. Here we are celebrating Christmas at our home in Glenmont, a suburb of Albany, 1992.

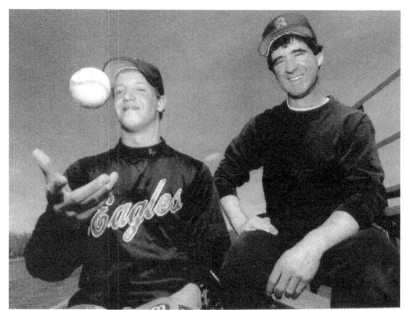

In 1994, a dream came true when I became coach of the Bethlehem Central High baseball team, the Eagles. Here I am, all smiles, with my star pitcher, Nate Kosoc in 1995.

The Eagles developed into a winning team, but the smiles didn't last. Here we are posing for a team photo in 1999, after we won the Section II championship. Things got dark soon after.

In the meantime I also founded my own summer Mickey Mantle team for young Bethlehem baseball aficionados. My pride and joy, the MM team also unfortunately—and unfairly—led to difficulties with the local authorities and my firing as BCHS varsity coach.

As luck—and the gods of baseball—had it I found a new home and "redemption" with the La Salle Cadets. Here we are, including our ace, Dave Roseboom (front row, third from right) celebrating our Section II championship at Joe Bruno

Stadium, Troy, in June 2008, at the end of our historic twenty-seven-game-winning season.

A number of my boys have fulfilled the dream I once had for myself, to play in the pros. Here I am with former Eagle Dan Conway (center) and his Colorado Rockies minor league teammate Cory Vance at 2002 spring training in Tucson, Arizona.

Cadet alumnus Dave Roseboom, now a pitcher with the Las Vegas Mets, is another one of "my" successful baseball grads.

Photo credit: Jennifer Nieves
Another chip off the old block, and former Eagle and Mantle player, Matt Quatraro, has gone on to coaching glory himself as hitting coach with the Cleveland Indians. Every summer I stop by Progressive Field to cheer him on.

I also continue to love to act. Here I am in the Classic Theater Guild's 2013 production of *A Christmas Story* at Proctors GE Theater, Schenectady, New York.

My "bench" is as strong as ever. Thirty years after we married, Debbie remains the love of my life.

My brother, Roger, a retired New York City junior high school physical education teacher, continues to have my back.

So does my best friend, Billy Rappaport. Here is Billy, now a surgeon in Arizona, with his wife and three boys.

I once was lost...Bethlehem High Central High, my
Gethsemane.

Looking out at Bethlehem field, scene of past glory—and sadness.

But now I am found. In front of La Salle. Who would think that a Jewish boy from Queens would reach his apotheosis at a Catholic school? True story.

In 2017 my alma mater, the University of Bridgeport, honored me by giving me its Fifth Annual Fran Bacon Award for Lifetime Achievement in Coaching. Here I am receiving the award from UB Athletic Director Anthony Vitti. *Photo credit: Regina Madwed, Capitol Photo Interactive*

Looking out at my revarnished field of dreams, Geer Field.

Jesse Jimmy, as my mentor Joe Austin used to call me, happy at last.

CHAPTER 6:
MR. B.

THE SUMMER of 1974 was an anxious one for me. Around the country Americans were fastened to their TV sets as they watched presidential counsel John Dean's riveting and ultimately damning testimony against his former boss, Richard Nixon, as the Watergate crisis—which would lead to Nixon's resignation the next month—came to its sorry conclusion.

As for myself, I was more consumed with the process and objective of finding a teaching job. I had never given much thought to living in the Capital District; however, Anna still had one year to go at Russell Sage College. Of course, I knew that I had to find a teaching position, and although I had done my best to do so, sending salvo after salvo of applications, the only job offers I had received thus far were from Elmira and Westchester, so it was beginning to look as if I might have to move out of the area and take a position elsewhere.

Although our first year of marriage had not been quite the oasis of joy we had envisioned, we were very much a couple and I remained completely committed to the relationship, a state of affairs that would shortly change.

In the meantime I had gone back to my default job as a doorman and elevator operator at a high-rise building on Sutton Place in Manhattan while I waited to see what the future would bring. Finally, on July first, the clouds broke and I received an appointment for an interview for a possible position as a middle school special education teacher at the Bethlehem School District in Delmar, a southwestern suburb of Albany, with Fred Burdick, the school principal, and Clarence Spain, the special education chair.

****

SEVERAL DAYS LATER, following my doorman shift, I hopped aboard the midnight bus from the Port Authority Bus Terminal bound for Albany for my interview, which I had scheduled early in the morning so I could return to Sutton Place the same day, where I was scheduled to work the same afternoon. I need not tell you that I didn't get much sleep.

Nevertheless the interview went well, as did a subsequent one with the district assistant superintendent, Briggs McAndrews, although of course one never knows how one actually fares in these situations. No sooner had I arrived back at Sutton Place that same day than I was informed by my fellow doorman that there was a call for me on the outside line: it was from Fred Burdick, the principal, offering me the position of middle school Resource Room Teacher with the Bethlehem Central School District in September. That was fast!

Everything was still going according to plan.

****

TWO MONTHS—and one presidential resignation—later, on September 4, 1974, I reported to the majestic edifice that was Bethlehem Middle School for my first day as Resource Room Teacher.

Little did I realize that I would spend a little more than three decades of my teaching career there; that I would begin a parallel, no less fulfilling, multi-sport athletic coaching career at Bethlehem; and that at the end I would be close to a broken man. For the moment, I was full of joy and energy, confident that luck and destiny, as well as my own hard work, had brought me to the right place.

Not that things were easy, by any means. As much as I believed in, and continue to believe in, the concept of mainstreaming—bringing a special needs student into a regular school—I found it difficult to adapt the regular curriculum to the needs of my students. I found that the curriculum was often too difficult, and, for the most part, inaccessible to my students, who though generally intelligent, were struggling with reading, writing, and basic math facts.

The entire array of assigned work, including homework, textbook readings, projects, and assignments, had to be adapted and modified to meet the special and unusual needs of my students, a formidable task indeed.

Another thing I discovered during my rookie year as a special ed teacher was the absolute necessity of first obtaining the cooperation of one's students. Without this, I quickly found, no learning could or would take place, and often as not it didn't, as I struggled to get my fractious students to listen to me.

Of course, this was par for the course for a rookie, but the experience could still be discouraging, as well as taxing of my patience, a character trait that I was not especially known for at the time. (Fortunately, that would change.)

All in all, my first months at Bethlehem were a very challenging time, as I felt and improvised my way through the minefield of pedagogical—and emotional—obstacles confronting a novice, twenty-two-year-old special ed instructor, no less one who still had some growing up of his own to do.

Assisting me in my apprenticeship was my fellow teacher, Diane Wallace, with whom I shared a small classroom, room 137, and in some cases, also co-taught classes. Unlike me, Diane had already had several years of experience under her belt teaching in Connecticut, and it showed. Although she was only several years older than me, she was already a consummate teacher.

Watching Diane work, I found myself amazed that this soft-spoken, calm, and gentle woman could be so firm while retaining control over her corner of the blackboard jungle without resorting to traditional disciplinarian methods. Simply by waiting patiently in front of an unruly class, this master teacher was able to quickly gain her students' attention and begin instruction.

Instead of broadcasting her authority, she *signaled* it through a finely tuned combination of body language, vocal inflection and command. By slightly ratcheting up the volume of her voice, Diane was able to signal to her students that they had crossed the line and had better calm down. They did.

Above all, Diane respected her students, and her students respected her, and so did I. I don't mind saying that I was in awe of Diane Wallace. She soon became my friend, confidante and mentor, and so she remains today. She also encouraged me to overcome whatever shyness or inhibitions I retained from my childhood—for I am, or at least used to be, a shy person—and *get in there* and mix it up with my students in as many different settings as possible. And yes, she also helped me in the patience area. I'm not quite sure whether I can call her the pedagogical equivalent of Joe Austin, but certainly she was close.

****

INEVITABLY I also found there were times when having the best education and best intentions, as well the most effective body language, as well as a fantastic mentor, were of little or no avail in dealing with my most difficult students.

Case in point: my first student, John.

Just before lunch, on my very first day as a teacher in September, 1974, a short, muscular, thirteen-year-old boy with wavy blond hair came barreling into my classroom and plunked himself into a seat in the front. Although I did my best to engage the late-arriving student in conversation, it was clear from the way John was cursing—evidently he had just had a run-in with his English teacher—and the way he was fidgeting around that he wouldn't be there for long.

I was right. After a few moments, John angrily stormed out of the room amidst a blue cloud of obscenities. After he exited, I ducked into the hall and called out his name, in vain. However, he was nowhere in sight. Talk about baptism by fire.

Somewhat flustered, I asked the class to excuse me and ran down to the school office a few doors down to report the unsettling incident.

"My student left my class," I told the school secretary, somewhat abashed. "Is he in the bathroom?" she chirped back. "No," I told the astonished woman, "I think he's left the building." And so he had. Shaking my head, I returned to the classroom, apologized to my students, and continued where I had left off.

Somehow I had a feeling that John would be a very challenging student, to say the least. So he would indeed prove to be. Sadly, John presented a challenge that I would ultimately lose, although I would never give up trying. More about John later.

****

FORTUNATELY, I would wind up winning more of the challenges that I faced as a novice special ed teacher during those early years than not.

First I had to overcome a challenge which I created for myself, namely my dual desire to teach and my passion to coach, which would also soon bear fruition. I recognized that my burgeoning coaching career could make me less available to provide the extra after-school help to a portion of the school population which could use all the help it could get!

So, shortly after my bifurcated coaching-cum-teaching career at Bethlehem Central began in earnest, I decided to resolve this problem, or potential problem, by coming to school *before* class, i.e., between 6:30 and 6:45 a.m., and making myself available to whomever showed up.

As it happened, quite a few students did. Before I knew it, five, six, seven, sometimes even a dozen students would be waiting for me when I arrived. The students' parents would drop them off on their way to work still with time to burn before homeroom began. Or, on occasion, if the students were lacking means of transport, I would pick them up myself.

As it turned out, my preferred morning help period proved extremely productive—much more so than my afterschool sessions. More often than not, the kids were generally calmer and more cooperative in the morning than in the afternoon. It was also a great way to start their day with a bang and help ensure that they were prepared for the day ahead. If this meant having to get up at 5 rather than 6:30, as I had been doing, this seemed a small price to pay for the joy and privilege of following in both of my mentors' footsteps—in Diane's, as an effective special education teacher, and Joe's, as a coach.

Moreover, my Sunday morning regimen at Harry and Midge's had trained me well for this sort of thing. To be sure, getting up and out at the crack of dawn also meant that Anna would see less of me, but if she minded she didn't say so. In fact she did. She minded even more the time I spent tutoring my students over the weekend, which also took away from our quality time.

Unquestionably a crack had developed in our young relationship, but I didn't see it. Bear in mind that we were still in our mid-twenties. And this was still several decades before *Dr. Phil.*

I would continue to offer my early morning help period for my special needs students for the duration of my rewarding—and challenging—career as a teacher at Bethlehem Central Middle School.

****

AS MUCH as I loved—and love coaching—I hasten to say that I have always considered myself a teacher first and a coach second. Although this memoir is primarily about my athletic coaching career, I should say that proud as I am of my coaching career, I am no less proud of my career as a special education teacher, as well as no less sure that my decision to devote myself to this vital, if misunderstood area of secondary education was the right one, even if I essentially stumbled into the field.

Years later, I also have some strongly held opinions about how this little understood field is taught, as well as, and particularly, about the no-less-misunderstood recipients of this recondite form of education.

To be sure, there are many misconceptions regarding learning-disabled students. One of the most common is that they are not bright. I can attest from my experience that this is not true. Another canard is that these children, who are as interested in learning as their learning-abled kinsmen, are "sloppy," or have no concept of or appreciation for what is exact or not.

False again. Perhaps the worst curse which has befallen many special needs students is that they are, in fact, perfectionists. If you want to see frustration up close and personal, try working with a student who has learning difficulties as well as high personal standards of perfection. The learning-disabled student is keenly, and often painfully, aware of his or her shortcomings. The student's "average" intelligence allows him or her to understand what "acceptable" schoolwork looks like.

Consequently, when these students fall short of this perceived standard, as they invariably do, an all-too-common reaction is to tear up the paper they had just been laboring over. "Perfect" becomes the enemy of the good. Feelings are hurt and re-engagement with the aborted assignment is more difficult. The fact that the students often *are* bright only makes their dilemma, as well as their teachers', more difficult.

I recall one such highly intelligent, learning disabled student—let's call him Mitchell—who lived a block from school and who was my student for two years in the mid-80s. Despite his intelligence, Mitchell struggled to read as much as any student I have had to work with. He also was highly motivated. Mitchell's intrinsic motivation convinced me that with time, effort, and perhaps a bit of creativity, it was possible to overcome his severe reading disability.

Fortunately, by this time, ten-odd years into my teaching career, I felt comfortable enough and was encouraged by the school authorities to *be* creative. From our conversations I learned that Mitchell had an impressive collection of comic books. This gave me an idea. Would he be willing to come in early every day and read from his prized books?

He would.

And so every day for the two years he was my student, Mitchell came to school and read from his comics.

It worked. I am pleased to say that today Mitchell is a registered nurse. Challenge met, challenge overcome.

****

AS the years went on, and I became more comfortable with teaching, I was able to use my imagination to help my students in other ways. Thus, later on in the 90s, I came up with the idea for a mentor program in which I would match a former student with a current one.

(Ironically, that idea was endorsed by the superintendent of the Bethlehem school district, with whom I would later clash over my concept of coaching and who would play a role in my firing and downfall, but that *contretemps* was still down the road.)

In one of my most successful mentor pairings, a current student, Seth (let's call him), was paired with ex-student Derek. As a student, although he had a learning disability, which evinced itself with the difficulty he had reading, Derek had possessed above average intelligence and was highly motivated. For the three years Derek was my student in the early 90s, he was in my classroom every morning at 7:00 am, diligently studying and working. He had since found employment as an administrative assistant in local government.

Seth was a less-than-conscientious student, with a significant learning disability in both reading and writing. Twice a week for three months Derek would help Seth understand and complete assignments for his eighth grade American history class. They would study together for unit tests and organize Seth's notebook, which badly needed it.

The arrangement worked well. Indeed it worked so well that Derek was inspired to become a teacher himself. Today, Derek is in his fifteenth year as a social studies teacher at an area high school. Challenge met, challenge overcome.

127

****

FOR ALL the misconceptions regarding learning-disabled students, there are just as many, if not more, about those who teach them. One of these is that teaching learning-disabled students is "easy." After all, an uninformed resource room visitor might wonder, how difficult can it be to teach four or five students, which is the norm?

What such visitors *don't* understand is that each of the "mere" four or five students sitting before them is learning—or trying to learn—something different. One student might be learning math, another science, yet another social studies, and so on. The fact that the students are sitting there quietly (hopefully), waiting for the teacher to get to them and continue with their individual subject matter, obscures the fact that the teacher is teaching not one class, but several, all at the same time.

Sometimes the teacher has an aide to assist him, sometimes not. In any case, I can assure you, the teacher's job is anything but "easy."

Another common misconception regarding special education relates to testing. In order to receive special education services in a public school, a student must meet certain psychological and educational criteria. Testing is the sole basis by which a particular school's Special Education Committee determines whether or not a student whose parents are applying for him or her to receive special education can qualify.

However, I can attest from experience that psychological testing cannot and does not tell the whole story, about an individual student. When teachers have a chance to inject their input into the process, more often than not their crucial testimony is wrongly—even criminally, in my opinion--dismissed as anecdotal.

As a result many, *too many* learning disabled students fall between the cracks.

I would like to think that my colleagues and I rescue some of them, but no matter how optimistic or committed we are, we can only do so much.

SUMMING up, my personal philosophy of special education can be boiled down to the following axioms:

1. Perseverance is everything.
2. Every student is unique.
3. Find the key to unlock each student's intrinsic motivation.
4. Listen.
5. Demonstrate the behaviors you want to develop in your students.
6. Build a relationship with the student's parents.
7. Match your instructional approach to each student's learning style.
8. Break down abstract and complex concepts into concrete examples.
9. Help students restrain impulsive behaviors in both learning and interpersonal situations.
10. Emphasize the importance of time and time management.
11. Be compassionate.

There it is: my mission statement as a teacher.

To be sure, I view my teaching and my coaching as two sides of the same humanistic coin. In both activities I was and am still a teacher. I think of my students and athletes as being quantitatively different, not qualitatively different. They are all young people developing their minds, bodies, and personalities, albeit at different rates.

I sincerely believe that being a special education teacher has made me a better coach, and being a coach has made me a better special education teacher.

And to think: special ed was my second choice. It certainly wound up being the right field at the right time for me—as well as, I would like to think, the thousand-odd learning-disabled students it has been my privilege to teach over the last forty-four years.

CHAPTER 7:
IN JOE'S FOOTSTEPS

IN THE SPRING of 1977, my third year at Bethlehem, I got my first shot at coaching, as well as to put what I had learned from Joe to use, when Ray Sliter, the Bethlehem athletic director, asked me whether I would like to coach the school's freshman girls' softball team.

Come again? Softball? Girls? I have to admit that I was a bit surprised. The notion of coaching women, no less at softball, had never even occurred to me.

Still, as one who enjoys new challenges, I decided to take it on.

It wasn't as hard a fit as I first thought. Unlike many of my more "macho" peers, I never had anything against the other sex. In fact, as far as men of that still relatively backward day and age were concerned, I considered myself relatively "liberated." My experience at the candy store, where the work that my mother did was virtually interchangeable with that of my father's, certainly helped me in this regard.

Joe himself had been relatively "liberated" as well in his own way, giving a number of local gals the opportunity to play in games.

OK. But *softball? SOFTBALL?!* Softball was nothing but a diluted, inferior form of baseball as far as Joe the purist was concerned. *Fuggedabout it.* The same went for stickball, an equally popular pastime back in the day in which I was known to indulge on occasion.

It didn't matter to Joe that many people who have played baseball in their youth eventually transition to softball. Softball was simply an ersatz form of baseball to him.

I could just imagine the sour expression that would have crossed his face if I had told him that I was considering coaching softball. So, on the odd occasion when I did see Joe when I returned to Jamaica, I never told him. I *did* tell Joe about my new career coaching girls' basketball. But I will get to that later.

Still, I am very glad that I accepted that challenge. In fact, over the following year I would also be asked and would accept the additional challenges of coaching two other women's teams, soccer and basketball. If, in my case, I was able to overcome my own ignorance of softball and soccer and become reasonably successful at coaching those sports, it was principally because of the quality, talent, and character of the young women I was fortunate enough to coach.

****

INDEED, now that I look back on it, the fact that I actually began my coaching career in women's sports, something of a novel experience unto itself, no less in three sports which I had little to no prior experience in and/or knew nothing or little about, i.e., softball, soccer, and basketball, turned out to be a blessing.

Suddenly, right at the start of my coaching career, I was inspired to develop an ecumenical *philosophy* that I could apply to *all* sports, *as well* as both genders, instead of focusing on tactics, as would have been the case if I had immediately starting coaching on the more familiar playing ground of baseball, as I had originally hoped.

Now I really had to think about the role of the coach *in general* and to formulate a set of *principles* that I could use in all three of these novel and challenging positions, while also postulating the sort of *athletes* I was trying to mold. This, in turn, better prepared me to coach men's baseball and men's sports when that opportunity came along eight years later.

Ultimately, I would wind up coaching roughly the same number of boys' teams as girls'—fifty-nine and fifty-eight respectively—but it is significant, I think, that the first "layer," or

132

template of my coaching career was formed in the relatively uncharted waters of women's sports, and for that I am very grateful—as well as for the experience of working with some of the finest athletes I have ever watched or coached.

Athletes. Who just *happened* to be women.

****

I'LL GET into the specifics of those coaching experiences, as well as some of the standout female softball, soccer and basketball players I worked with during those eye-opening, pulse-pounding formative years in a moment.

But first I would like to share the coaching philosophy and those principles that wound up guiding me during the rest of my coaching career.

And if some of them sound familiar, don't be surprised:

1. Reinforce commitment, as well as performance.

2. Play to win, but as humanely as possible.

3. In a close game, those with the most ability and strongest work ethic will play the most, but if the team is comfortably ahead or hopelessly behind, then playing time will be divided as equally as possible.

4. Listen to parents but don't be intimidated by them.

5. If you have to gloat, gloat in private.

6. Engage with the local community.

7. Always be there for your players.

8. Girls can do anything boys can.

9. Come to the field or court prepared to play and play hard. Or don't come at all.

10. Never give up on a player no matter how helpless he or she may seem.

11. Keep your sense of humor: after all, it *is* only a game.

****

TRUTH BE TOLD, I had little or no idea what to expect when I took charge of the Bethlehem freshmen softball team, the

Lady Eagles, in the spring of 1977, three years after I began teaching at Bethlehem: I deliberately waited until I received tenure before I took up my first coaching assignment.

And a challenging assignment it was: I had never even *seen* a girls' softball game played before.

It turned out to be a more fruitful and enjoyable experience than I had anticipated, largely because of the quality and character of the players I had the privilege to coach. Bill Parcells, the legendary New York Giants football coach, once was asked after his second Super Bowl victory in 1991 what he attributed his success to. He replied: "I had good players."

I could say the same thing about my first team, the 1977 freshman softball team. Much to everyone's surprise—including and especially my own—the girls managed to go undefeated, this in a league that was considered to be extremely competitive.

Technically, I was able to transfer very little from my baseball experience to my softball experience. Ironically, the aspect of baseball that I would have been most comfortable teaching—pitching—was the area of softball I knew absolutely nothing about. Fortunately, I had an ace of a pitcher in the form of Mary Gardner, a righty with short blonde hair and a killer arm.

Our catcher, Molly Nevins, who caught for Mary—in softball fortunately one can use the same pitcher in every game—played every bit as physically as a boy. She had rare upper body strength for a female and hit the ball with real authority. Behind the plate, she was like a brick wall; absolutely *nothing* got by her.

Molly's enthusiasm was absolutely contagious. In a way she was the female equivalent of Thurman Munson, the hard-charging catcher who was then the heart and soul of the New York Yankees, albeit without Munson's moustache or his temper: a true leader on and off the field. As a softball catcher, she could absolutely do it all, catching, throwing, and blocking as well as just about any baseball catcher I have ever seen.

Fortunately, I *was* able to provide good instruction in the *other* non-pitching aspects of the game, i.e., hitting, bunting, fielding, and base running. *Too* good as far as some of the girls were concerned. When, channeling my inner Joe Austin, I would hit

134

high fungo pop-ups during our infield drills, sometimes the girls would complain, "Hey Mr. Braverman, no one hits them that high in the game."

To which I would cheerily reply: "*Good*, then the game should be easy." Perhaps Joe might not have been pleased with the setting, but he would have approved of the message, which I would also convey in various forms in the seventy other coaching assignments I would ultimately take on at Bethlehem, including with both genders.

I think, however, that during my first outing of coaching women I never thought that I was coaching girls, but rather *female athletes*. As it happened, I started coaching women at the same time that Title IX, the federal act mandating equal funding for both men's and women's sports went into effect. I have to admit that I wasn't especially focused on Title IX and didn't realize how much of a watershed event it was for the world of high school and college sports; if it had any effect on me, it was only subliminal.

In any event, my "all players are athletes" attitude came into play in a memorable, somewhat controversial, and pivotal game that we played in my first season against the high school in Burnt Hills, a suburb north of Schenectady. Their team was the closest to us, both in terms of ability and record.

When we faced Burnt Hills in April, 1977, our record was 6 and 0, while theirs was 5 – 1. As it happened, the contest was held at their elementary school, as these sorts of contests often are, making for a somewhat incongruous setting for the mayhem that transpired.

The very unladylike fracas, one of the most disturbing events of my entire career, took place during the third inning of the game, when we were leading 6 to 4 before a crowd of about seventy onlookers, virtually all of them Burnt Hills partisans. At the time we had runners on first and second with none out. Up at the plate was another member of our "murderer's row," Mary Cannizaro, a big strong player who could handle a bat as well as any guy.

With the Burnt Hills infield playing back, I gave Mary the bunt sign. She responded just the way I taught her, expertly laying the ball down the third base line and forcing the Burnt Hills third baseman to come in and field it. The surprised third baseman's only possible play was to first base, however her errant throw was down the first base line toward home plate, pulling the Burnt Hills first baseman off the bag and down the line and causing a painful, major-league-caliber collision between Mary and the unfortunate first baseman.

Unsurprisingly, both girls were badly shaken up. However, the first baseman got the worst of it, as is often the case, but fortunately no bones were broken. Naturally, I was concerned: no sane coach likes to see his player or the opposing ones hurt, no less in softball. However, I have to say, I was even more upset when the umpire, who obviously had a sketchy knowledge of the sport, decided to call Mary out for interference, the exact opposite of the correct ruling.

I was not going to take this lying down. As calmly as I could, I tried to explain to the unenlightened umpire that a runner could only interfere with a fielder on a batted ball, and not a thrown one that was well wide of the base.

Cue fireworks. Not only did I get nowhere with the umpire, but the partisan Burnt Hills crowd saw my arguing as disrespectful of the injured player. It didn't help matters, I suppose, when I angrily and audibly proclaimed that the players preferred to be treated as athletes, rather than as girls.

The crowd—including, presumably, some of the home team players' boyfriends—decided to make its displeasure known by throwing stones and other objects at our girls. A full scale riot was at hand, or so it seemed. I immediately ordered my team, who were naturally frightened and upset, to come off the field and stay on the team bus and remain there until the umpires could restore order.

If anything the incident strengthened our players' resolve. When the game resumed, we opened up a huge lead, to the continued loud displeasure of the Burnt Hills fans, and coasted to victory by the score of 19 – 6.

The next day, Ray Sliter, the Bethlehem athletic director, stopped by my classroom. He said that he had received a distressed call from his Burnt Hills counterpart inquiring about the identity of the coach of the Bethlehem freshman softball team. "Who is that guy you have," he asked, *Billy Martin?*" referring to the Yankees' famously combative then-manager and one-time second baseman.

Ray didn't tell me how he responded; however, I gather from his bemused expression that he understood the principle involved: the rules for female players were the same as for male ones. The umpire had been dead wrong. And, of course, the reaction of the Burnt Hills fans had been unspeakable.

To be sure, I have had run-ins with other umpires who have been wrong since then, and have managed to better control my temper, but I don't apologize for my reaction to that bad call that day, and never have. And I imagine if that roughed-up first baseman had had any say in the matter, she would have backed me up, too.

****

MY MAIDEN season of coaching women's softball concluded with the first of many Joe Austin-inspired parties I would have for each of the seventy-two teams in both women's and men's sports I would ultimately coach at Bethlehem. One night in early June the entire team descended on the Bravermans' garden apartment in Troy.

To this day, I still cherish the memory of my kneeling on the carpet in the middle of our living room, surrounded by the exultant members of the 1977 freshman girls' softball team, presenting each girl with an individually engraved trophy, just the way Joe always used to do for us in bygone Emerald days. The party was a lot of fun, and set a template for future end-of-season parties.

I'd like to think that Anna also enjoyed herself, although I can't say for sure. I have to confess that I was not giving her as much time and attention as she deserved—and certainly not as much as Anna, who was no longer interested in becoming an art therapist and was now tinkering with the idea of becoming an interior designer, would have liked.

****

AT THIS POINT, several years into our marriage, I was aware that there were cracks in our relationship, but I presumed that we would be able to fix them. Little did I realize that those cracks would become fissures. Although I loved Anna, perhaps selfishly, my focus continued to be on my blossoming parallel teaching and coaching careers.

Ultimately, I would remain with the BC softball program for another seven years, through 1984, and even though I would have preferred to teach baseball, I loved every minute of it.

I was blessed with many terrific players and teams during that time. Our teams' strengths were defense, bunting, base-running, and putting the ball in play consistently. I was also pleased to see our teams make frequent and effective use of two of my signature plays, the squeeze play and the hit and run.

I was blessed with many great players. A very incomplete list of my standouts would include Kelly and Karen Burke, Judy and Janet Vanwoert, Jill Kaplowitz, Leeane Cory, Mary Malone, Leanne Stokoe, Mary Nyllis, Julie Liddle, Laura Guevara, Kris VanAernam, Debbie Pangburn, Barbara Cebry, Lauren, Kathy and Alesia Harder, Laurie Weinert, Shelly Richter, Jackie Cozzy, and Laurie Riccardo, and of course, Molly Nevins.

Amongst the novel experiences I had that first spring of my coaching career was the Spring Sports Banquet, which in those days was held for every sport in the high school cafeteria. This would be my first of many such public speaking engagements, and not necessarily the most successful. As I have given more of these addresses over the years I have also become more adept at combining recognition of the student-athletes with a few humorous anecdotes.

However, this time, I have to say, the laugh was on me. The risible part came when I was describing one of our top hitters,

Janet Vanwoert, who had managed twenty-eight hits in only thirty-four at bats. Thus when the time came for me to praise Janet for her exemplary performance at the plate, I noted, in referring to her feat, "As you can gather, Janet was not making out often."

Whereupon, to my befuddlement, the audience suddenly broke into hilarious laughter. After a confused pause I continued with my speech. It was only after I sat down and asked one of the other coaches what everyone was laughing at that I finally understood, and had my own belated, embarrassed laugh.

As it happened Janet was not in the audience that night; however, I am reasonably sure that if she was, she would have gotten the joke as well.

****

ULTIMATELY, looking back on my career as a coach of women's sports, I would like to think that I learned as much from my girls as they did from me.

I certainly learned that female athletes are no better nor worse than their male counterparts. They are simply different.

Amongst other things, I also learned that because female athletes' egos tend not to be as invested in their on-field performance as is normally the case with male athletes, they generally have an easier time accepting a loss, or, as in the case of the aforementioned banquet *faux pas,* taking an unintended joke.

Would Janet have laughed along with the audience after my miscue if she were a boy? I am not so sure. As the French say, *Vive la différence!*

****

AS IT turned out, I barely had the chance to savor my unlikely "success" coaching women's softball, when, in the fall of that pivotal year of 1977, I was given the even more formidable challenge of coaching women's soccer.

139

Soccer! What did I know about soccer? I knew less about soccer than I did softball. Nevertheless, when Ray Sliter, the BCHS athletic director, and Vicki Bylsma, the long-time varsity girls' soccer coach, double-teamed me and asked me smilingly whether I would be willing to also coach the junior varsity soccer team, I had a hard time saying no.

Why not? I said to myself. Anything for BCHS. Still, soccer? What did I know about soccer? Perhaps I had caught one or two glimpses of the New York Cosmos, who were then on their way to winning their third North American Soccer League championship, with the aid of Pele, the aging but still redoubtable Brazilian import.

Still, soccer? I was not even remotely familiar with the rules of this exotic sport, let alone the techniques and skills I was expected to imbue upon my eager players.

Why not? Coach Can Do, as I liked to consider myself, insisted. Why not.

"Okay," I told Ray and Vicki, after a long second or two, "I will give it a try." If only I had known…

****

WHAT DID I *do*? I kept asking myself during the few short weeks remaining before the season kicked off that August. I certainly made no effort to hide my lack of experience. I eagerly sought the advice and counsel of anyone who knew anything about what was still an exotic sport on this side of the Atlantic. Remember, these were still the days when most Americans hadn't even heard of the World Cup, let alone knew the winner of the last one.

Thankfully, Vicki let me stay close during the first few days of the season while the varsity and junior varsity rosters were being determined, which allowed me to get a rough handle on the game and helped me figure out whom to assign positions. Still, I dreaded the September day when tryouts would be concluded and I would be on my own.

Soon enough, September and the dreaded first game arrived. On that late summer afternoon, two days after Labor Day in 1977, I received my baptism by fire as a soccer coach as I watched my disorganized team re-enact the Brownian movement from the sidelines. Clearly, many of the girls lacked the necessary skills to execute successful strategy. Some of them barely seemed to understand the basics of the game. Neither did I.

Fortunately, in addition to Vicki, who had been coaching the varsity team since the late 60s and had gained a reputation as a respected physical education teacher and soccer coach, I also had another informal mentor in the person of one Mr. Castle (I never did catch his first name), the coach of Bethlehem's excellent club soccer team and the father of one of our team leaders. From him I learned how to run a soccer practice and the basic principles of game strategy.

More importantly, Mr. Castle provided invaluable instruction in soccer fundamentals, especially the techniques needed to achieve proficiency in basic skills. Next, he provided me with a collection of drills to develop individual and team play. Mr. Castle was the first of a long line of people, including coaches and parents, who helped me learn the rudiments of *futbol*.

I soon learned that I had to place my most skilled players, who were able to settle and control the ball, on defense rather than up front in a futile attempt to score goals. I also learned that the most talented players, who were athletic and versatile, were best employed in the middle of the field where they would be able to use their ability to control the game. Mr. Castle also introduced me to team tactics, such as diagonal defensive support and overlapping runs of offense. I learned the value of "switching the ball" as well as the pitfalls of turning the ball to the middle and retreating.

My first season as the coach of the Bethlehem JV Girls Soccer Team was nothing short of on-the-job training. The team clearly struggled, but as I became more knowledgeable about the game, our performance clearly improved. I realized there was more to coaching soccer than merely throwing the ball on the field and blowing a whistle. Imagine that.

Surprisingly given my limited soccer background, we usually finished in the top half of the league. Even more surprisingly I wound up coaching JV soccer for another twenty-three years!

Back in the late 70s, when I began coaching soccer, the Suburban Council, the upstate New York school region to which Bethlehem belonged, was divided into two six-team divisions. The Bethlehem JV Girls Soccer Team finished in the top half of its division and the entire league in two thirds of my seasons as coach. In 1990, we won a division championship, and in 1994 and 1999, we were the top JV team in the entire Suburban Council.

I would like to think that I had something to do with our success; however, the greater part of our wins can be attributed to the spirit and abilities of the girls I was fortunate to coach, along with the support I received from the girls' parents and Mr. Castle.

I also honed my philosophy of how to manage team members' playing time. Unlike baseball or softball, soccer allows for free substitution. In other words, new players can enter and re-enter the game an unlimited number of times. While athletes who had both exceptional talent and a strong work ethic received the largest share of playing time, I was also able to rotate into the game players with less skill and experience. This shared approach to playing time proved a vital ingredient in the development of optimum team chemistry.

In 1981, my JV soccer team was led by a remarkable athlete, Terry Plunkett. Terry quickly established herself as a magnificent player with prodigious strength, capable of scoring a goal from anywhere inside of forty yards. She single-handedly avoided defeat by division powerhouse Shenendehowa for the first time in my coaching tenure with a hat trick, scoring all three goals in a thrilling 3 – 3 tie.

That year the team was also blessed with a sure-handed and agile goalkeeper, Yolanda Smith. Four games into the season, the team's record stood at 3 – 0 – 1 when the varsity goalie sustained a serious injury. As often happens to a JV team, this meant we would be losing our anchor.

142

1981 was also a year in which I acquired valuable experience in dealing with players who faced personal challenges that often compromised their judgment and attitude. Case in point: that year we had a problematic player who I will call Harriet. Harriet had personal issues and frequently exhibited discipline problems in school. She certainly had legitimate soccer talent, but she was the sort of person many of my fellow coaches urged me not to keep because of her poor attitude and influence.

On the day the team learned it would be losing Yolanda to the varsity, Harriet was late to practice. The girls were understandably upset about being treated as a farm team for the varsity. Harriet arrived about forty-five minutes late, having just been released from detention. As usual, she was irritable when I asked for an explanation for her tardiness. I explained to her that Yolanda was being promoted to varsity. I told her the team was not happy, and if she was in a bad mood, to please keep it to herself because her attitude was contagious.

"If you don't like it, you can lump it," Harriet responded.

I replied, "I prefer to lump it today. Why don't you just go home and come back tomorrow in a better frame of mind."

Harriet stormed off, declaring, "If I leave, I'm never coming back."

"That's not what I said," I told her, "but it's up to you." That seemed to do the trick.

The next day, not only did Harriet return, but she agreed to become the new goalie. There were still tumultuous times ahead—at one point she received a yellow card for unsportsmanlike conduct—but she played well enough in goal for the team to allow us to finish the 1981 season with a record of nine wins, four losses, and three draws.

****

IN ADDITION to learning how to deal with difficult players, coaching the junior varsity soccer team also helped me acquire the no less (if not more) valuable skill of dealing with difficult parents.

143

It was difficult to keep everyone happy. There were games where I erred on the side of trying to give everyone equal playing time and upset some parents, and there were games where I erred on the side of trying to win.

In 1987 Ray asked me if I wanted to coach varsity soccer, which by then had seen *six* coaches come and go over the prior *ten* seasons, to a large degree because of the difficulty they had dealing with parents.

In any case, Ray thought he would do better with me. I thought otherwise and told him flatly, "I don't know anything about soccer."

Ray's response was somewhat annoyed. "You have been doing it for ten years," he declared.
Don't you know anything by now?"

"I know enough to know where I belong," I responded. To Ray's credit, he respected that. I remained JV coach and would continue to do so for another fourteen years, amassing a respectable record of 215 – 118 – 20 (to the best of my recollection).

****

AS IF I DIDN'T already have enough on my plate, in November 1978, a year after taking on the tremulous challenge of coaching soccer, a sport I knew nothing about, Ray approached me with another request: would I possibly consider *also* coaching JV basketball? This time, by way of a Greek chorus, Ray was accompanied by Briggs McAndrews, the BHCS assistant superintendent, and Ken Hodge, the varsity coach.

Evidently, along with my growing reputation as BCHS's resident Coach Can Do, my qualified success with softball and soccer had persuaded them that I was the person for this post, as well.

I could do that, I thought. After all, this was a sport that I knew *something* about. Although as a kid, baseball had always been my first love, basketball was a close second. I had played innumerable pick-up games in the old 131 schoolyard with Bruce

Lerro over the years. I was also a devoted fan of the sport and had attended droves of Knicks games at Madison Square Garden. "Hoops," I thought. "Can do."

However, as I soon discovered, when push comes to shove (as it literally does in basketball), in the end, being a fan of a sport means very little. That basic truth was driven home to me in my very first game, when I used timeouts to stem my opponents' momentum. The game, against Colonie High School, turned out to be close and I found myself with no timeouts remaining in the last ten minutes as the clock wound down in my first, losing contest. So much for my expert knowledge of basketball, or bball, as we also used to call it.

One person who was decidedly unhappy with my decision to take on this new athletic mantle was my wife Anna, who was already upset with the long hours I put in teaching and coaching. "Can't you ever say no?" she exclaimed when I told her (or words to that effect).

No, I guess I couldn't.

Matters were not helped by Anna's failure to find a career into which she could pour herself—at the time she was working at an Ethan Allen outlet in Schenectady—and her tendency to isolate herself. She was also becoming progressively lonelier and was prone to anxiety attacks.

The purchase of an expansive—too expansive, it turned out—four-bedroom home in Averill Park in September of 1979 did not help matters either. It was only a matter of time before our rickety edifice of a relationship collapsed, although I was too busy, or perhaps too young, to see it.

Back to the court…

Fortunately, as was the case with soccer, I did have an excellent mentor in the person of Ken Hodge, the able varsity coach. I also learned that as JV coach I was actually part of two games—the JV and the varsity—and that I was expected to be present for the latter on the bench, as well as coach the former.

Truth be told, I don't remember very much about my first season coaching basketball, other than spending a lot of time with Ken watching the courtside action and diligently trying to absorb what he did. In this way, I gradually acquired the basics of strategy, including the most common offenses and defenses. At practice after school I followed Ken's lead by employing drills designed to teach individual and team skills.

Although I knew something about the game I was still essentially a beginner, as I made clear to my players and their parents. In any event, I don't recall there being too many complaints.

I do recall one humorous incident that took place in the spring at a varsity game while I was sitting on the bench looking on. I was avidly following the action one night in February of 1979 when suddenly one of our players, by the name of Lisa, suddenly ran off the court in the middle of the action and made a beeline for the exit door. Suddenly our hardy band of five sisters had been reduced to four.

What was that all about, Ken and I wondered, scratching our heads.

A minute or two later Lisa reappeared at the door and ran back to the court, as if nothing was amiss. "Sorry coach," she said to Ken as she made her way her back, with a slightly flushed face, "but my bra snapped."

Obviously, I still had a lot to learn about women's sports!

My second season coaching JV basketball in 1979 stands more readily in my mind for several reasons.

For one, it provided me with my first opportunity to work with a great basketball player by the name of Sandy Shelmerdine, a sophomore. Driving to the basket, dribbling, passing, rebounding—there was nothing this gifted BCHS sophomore could not do on the court. Her lightning-quick hands and feet were a vision to behold.

When I think of Sandy on defense, I am reminded of an observation someone once made about Walt "Clyde" Frazier, the great New York Knicks player who was then at his dervish-like peak. Referring to Frazier's preternatural ability to whip the ball away from his flabbergasted opponents, Knicks teammate Dave Stallworth said of him, "He could steal the hubcaps off a moving car."

So could Sandy Shelmerdine—although she doubtless would have blanched at the analogy.

All in all, Sandy was the consummate player and athlete, as well as a role model for the team. Thanks to her inspired play, the JV basketball team amassed a formidable 17 – 3 record, and the best in the twelve-member Suburban Council league.

Thanks to Sandy's ferocious play, as well as Ken's continued help, I also fell into the groove. I also found that basketball, unlike soccer, was an excellent outlet for my own innate intensity. Of course, I still had a lot to learn about basketball, women's sports, and women in general, as I was fast discovering in both my on and off-the-court life. However, by the time 1980 spring season rolled around I could say that I was coaching three sports at the same time. How many twenty-eight-year-old high school coaches could say that?

****

PROUD as I was of this milestone, I didn't have much time to gloat, because the end of that basketball season also coincided with the breakup of my marriage. By this time, six years into our marriage, I was of course aware of the widening fissures in our relationship, as well as Anna's continued unhappiness with my ever-widening tray of coaching duties. I would have been deaf, dumb, and blind not to be.

Matters were not helped by tensions between me and my wife's family, the less said about which the better. Nevertheless, when the end finally came it was a tremendous shock.

It was on March 29, 1980, a day which is still indelibly engraved in my memory, that Anna walked out on me. Perhaps Bethlehem Central loved Coach Can Do, but my wife didn't anymore, or so she said as she huffed off.

All of a sudden, at the age of twenty-eight, I was alone watching television in our now cavernously empty four-bedroom house. The good feelings which attended the excellent start of what would turn out to be a successful forty-one-year coaching career paled next to the yawning chasm of my personal life, and I fell into the first of a number of rolling depressions.

Somehow I managed to get through the rest of the horrible term. However, when the final school bell rang at the end of that tumultuous year, I knew that there was no way that I could last the summer alone, so, as the Beatles used to sing, I decided to go back to where I once belonged—back home to Jamaica, to the reassuring embrace of my parents and my mother's home cooking, and, to the sanctuary of the old field and playing for Joe.

****

NEEDLESS to say, my parents were happy to see me. No questions asked, my parents helped right my ship.

For his part, my late blooming father, Harry, now in his sixties, had made tremendous strides in righting his own ship. Freed from the stress and strife of managing a candy store, he had by now found a secure job in the microfilm department of Bear Stearns, the stock brokerage, and was even taking senior citizen courses at Touro College.

As always, his principal worry—as well as mine and Roger's—continued to be my mother, who, despite being diagnosed and treated for hyperthyroidism, continued to experience extreme mood swings and was essentially confined to home. Still, the key thing was that she was *there*.

And now, for better or worse, so was I.

And then there was Joe. Joe was sitting on a folding chair next to the old bench behind Jamaica High when I returned that memorable day in June, 1980. Just like old times, he was using a stub of a pencil to scratch out that day's lineup.

I could see that his clientele had changed somewhat. Now the field was teeming with Hispanic children. The old man's sky blue eyes sparkled when he saw me approach. "Jesse Jimmy!"—his favorite nickname for me—he called out.

"Hi Joe! You need a guy on the mound?" I asked. Without hesitation, Joe began to pencil my name on his lineup. "Jesse Jimmy welcome to the Muchos Amigos!"

148

Who says that you can't go home again.

To be sure, although over a decade had passed since I had spent much time with Joe, I found him to be the same, loving, caring man around his kids, except that now most of them were Hispanic. No problem. As long as they gave it their all, Joe didn't care. Now in his seventies and saddled with a bum knee, Joe was clearly not the same man he used to be. Hence the folding chair. Nevertheless, remarkably he still managed to get to the field every day.

I did not go into great detail with Joe about my split with Anna and why I had suddenly shown up. In fact, I don't think I mentioned it all. Basically, I just showed up

Over time I did give Joe a selected update on my coaching career. I told him that I had begun to coach basketball, which he seemed to approve of. I didn't mention soccer or softball.

Joe was just happy that I was there, and so was I. And that, basically, was that. Every day that summer I showed up, just like old times, and every day I played. Once a week I even took the mound. Looking out at the field before I took my windup, through half-closed eyes I swear that it could still have been 1964 or 1968, and not 1980. The only difference was that I was, well, older. Who says you can never go home again? For that one transitional summer, the summer of 1980, I certainly did.

Unfortunately, as I could also see when my eyes refocused, my septuagenarian mentor was aging as well. Now aged seventy-six, he was definitely showing signs of aging and had slowed down considerably, which was painful for me. He now spent more time sitting on his portable bench or folding chair on the side of the pepper field, and less hitting his patented fungos.

But that was okay.

And so the summer of 1980 passed.

I can't say that I was completely healed by the time September rolled around. However, the combination of being home in the place that for me, has always been home, and playing for Joe certainly accelerated the healing process.

And of course I was sustained by the prospect of returning to my teaching duties and coaching my girls.

149

Returning to Albany, I rented out the three vacant bedrooms of my house, which provided a welcome source of income, as well as companionship, inasmuch as I was able to go through the motions of being the friendly host in my still somewhat discombobulated state.

I also began seeing a psychiatrist, which helped to a degree.

However, as always, the best therapy—at least for me—was getting back to work.

In any event, it is fair to say that 1980 was not my favorite year.

****

1981, the year I turned thirty, was a definite improvement.

One of the reasons was my somewhat impetuous, but sound decision to return to the theater. Someone who didn't know me might have said that I was mad to take on this additional commitment beyond my already formidable teaching and coaching duties. Anna certainly would have if she had been around. But she wasn't.

Although there were and would continue to be times when my cat's cradle of commitments and activities would be a source of anxiety to me, the fact is I have always been happiest—or in this case, when I was recovering from a traumatic personal experience—less depressed, when I was my busiest. To be sure, there is a fine line between a teacher/coach who can do it all, and one who is doing too much, and, I found, I would often cross it.

In any case, my decision to return to the theater proved an inspired one. It happened rather quickly. One day in April, 1981, while glancing through *The Albany Times Union,* I saw an open call for a local production of *The Good Doctor*, a comedy with music by Neil Simon which was at the Albany Civic Theater. Not one of Simon's best-known efforts, *The Good Doctor* comprises a series of eight short plays by the great Russian dramatist Anton Chekhov, each framed by a writer making comments on them.

"This looks interesting," I said to myself. Not that I was a Chekhov aficionado by any means. All I knew about Chekhov was that he was dark, and funny, which suited my current mood fine. In the end I wound up being cast in two of the Chekhovian vignettes—*The Surgery*, in the part of a young dentist who is a little too invested in his profession, and *The Arrangement*, in which the writer recalls the time his father took him to a house of ill repute as a rite of passage.

In the same way that it had felt good to be back on the mound, so it was to be back on the boards.

Who says you can't go home again?

To my great pleasure and delight, *The Good Doctor* was a great success, playing for eight performances over two weekends. That gratifying and uplifting experience led to my being offered and accepting other offers to appear in various theater productions in the Albany area.

Also, unexpectedly, and no less welcome, my reengagement with the theater also proved restorative in other ways, leading directly to my first post-separation relationship with one of my fellow castmates, and then, when that Chekhovian liaison ran its course, to another more serious and longer lasting one with a fan of the production who also saw me in the play and decided to pursue me.

I guess I was moving on. However, though we were having fun, I knew I hadn't found the right one.

****

IN the meantime, I continued to have fun and reasonable success coaching JV basketball. My 1981 team had a respectable 14 – 6 record. Next year, 1982, our final tally was 13 – 7.

In 1983, as a result of my qualified success with the JV team, Ray asked me whether I would be willing to switch to coaching the Lady Eagles freshman basketball team. As was my wont, I agreed with alacrity, as this would enable me to coach in the middle school where I taught.

Once again I did well, partly because of my luck in finding wonderful players, first and foremost of whom was Anita Kaplan. Walking through the sixth grade corridor one day in the fall of 1985, I was startled to see a girl protruding above the crowd who

151

must have been six feet tall. Upon inquiring, the young lady in question told me that her name was Anita Kaplan.

"Anita," I asked, "do you play basketball?"

"Not really," my young find replied. As a sixth grader, of course, Anita was not eligible for freshman basketball. Thinking quickly, I asked her whether she would consider becoming team manager, which would enable her to play with the team, if not yet play for it. After a moment, she shyly agreed.

My hunch about Anita turned out to be correct. I found her to be intelligent and extremely conscientious. She diligently took part in all drills during the first half of practice, working to develop her personal shooting and other skills. During the second half, when team tactics were our focus, Anita would duly separate from the team and continue working out on her own.

All in all, Anita was a marvel to behold. The team might be working on our press break[6] at one end of the gym, while on the other there would be Anita banging away until she made her personal quota of converting one hundred left-handed layups.

Once she entered seventh grade, the following year, my prospect became a fully-fledged and enthusiastic team player. Like other young athletes who have grown unusually tall or in some other way experienced an unusual physical surge, it was still a challenging time for Anita, as she struggled to develop her coordination. However, she still managed to make a major contribution to the team, scoring fifty-four points and pulling down eighty rebounds as we caromed to a more than respectable 11 – 3 season.

The following year, 1986-87, Anita joined the varsity and did even better there, more than fulfilling my expectations of her. My loss was new varsity coach Gene Lewis's gain. Ultimately, Anita went on to garner a four-year basketball scholarship to Stanford University and played a pivotal role on the Stanford's 1992 National Championship team. Deciding to stay with the sport,

---

[6] Press break: an offensive strategy designed to combat full-court defensive pressure.

she actually went on to play professionally in Europe for four years in Italy, France, and Sweden.

All in all, I am very glad that I spotted Anita Kaplan strolling the sixth-grade corridor back in1985, and I suspect that she is too.

****

DURING the interim, I also liked to think that I was becoming more proficient at the sport itself, including learning how much impact I as a coach could have on the outcome of a game, provided I knew what I was doing.

By 1986-7, my eighth season coaching basketball, I believe I did. It also helped to have another superstar, in this case an explosive eighth grader named Julie Francis.

Witness the explosive conclusion of our final game against then-undefeated Shenendehowa in February, 1987. With a 9 – 4 record, we had already been doing well, but we were still very much in the shadows of Shenendehowa, whose record was 13 – 0.

The Shenendehowa coach, an older woman named Gina, apparently had taken a dislike to me, as unavoidably happens once in a while. I inferred that she was annoyed at the level of "unladylike" competitiveness I brought to the court.

Not that she had much to worry about: in eight seasons of playing against her, my JV and freshman teams had notched exactly one win.

In any case, Gina didn't think she had much to worry about. Encountering me before the game, she sniffed, "It looks like we are going to go undefeated this year." Her confidence about the result was bolstered by the fact that the four games we had lost had all been to teams who Gina's girls had easily disposed of.

Talk about a red flag! "I thought we had one more game to play," I sniffed back, my fighting spirit further aroused.

For the game, I decided to take advantage of our team's speed and employ an aggressive man-to-man defense. Of all of my coaching experiences, there are few instances that come to mind which match the excitement of a closely contested basketball game. This game was one of them. Unfortunately, in this case we were losing.

Time to put my coach's cap on.

With 4:09 remaining in the game, and trailing 26 – 19, it was clear that the strategy I had decided on had taken us as far as it could. Sometimes, I had learned, teams have problems adjusting to a change in defense, as was evidently the case here. Quickly taking stock, I decided to use one of my remaining timeouts— happily by this juncture I had learned *not* to use all of my timeouts—and had the girls go into a half-court trap,[7] a defense which we had successfully used before, if not against a team of Shen's caliber.

Right move, it turned out. With Julie taking the lead, the girls now proceeded to go on to a 7 – 0 run and tied the score at 26 as the clock ran down in the fourth quarter. After a missed shot by Shen, we gained possession with five seconds remaining. Now Aileen Burke, one of our dependable players, dribbled around her defender.

If there had been a play by play commentator, this is how he might have sounded….

"One second on the clock….and here comes Burke…driving…driving…and here's her layup…and…it's in—and there's the buzzer. Game to Bethlehem! Pandemonium on the court as Burke is mobbed by her jubilant teammates. And in the middle of the joyous scrum is Coach Jesse Braverman…"

As it happened, there was no commentator to broadcast our resounding achievement, nor any journalist of any kind—not even one from the school paper. In fact, the only person to witness our feat other than the respective coaches and players, including the duly chagrinned Shenendehowa coach, was our loyal scorekeeper, Mike.

Fair enough.

Now *that* was a game to remember.

Tell me that women can't do what men can.

----

[7] Half-court trap: when players on a team double-team the dribbler when they cross the half-court line.

CHAPTER 8:
JOHN

I was a foster mother to a teenage boy back in the 1970s. I had many problems with him from time to time, but with the help of a dedicated teacher, Jesse Braverman, my job was easier...

—from a letter from Leona, John's late foster mother, published in *The Spotlight*, an Albany-area newspaper, on April 25, 2001.

IT HAS been said that the one absolute requirement for a successful teacher is a resilient and unshakeable optimism. On the basis of my forty-four years of experience as a special education teacher, I can say that this is doubly true for a teacher of special needs students.

Inevitably there are times when this axiom is tested, and perhaps found wanting. Sometimes, as many of you teachers who are reading this know, sometimes what you do isn't enough.

Case in point: my aforementioned "incorrigible" student, John. Yes, the same John who was my first student, the same one who had "escaped" from my first classroom all the way back in 1974, when I was starting out.

As I discovered, my initial, unsettling experience with John heralded many more difficult years to come, including the two years when he was one of my charter resource room students. Although John was intelligent, his basic reading and math skills were lacking—no doubt the result of his not being engaged in the learning process.

It was not difficult to understand why. To say that John was a hard luck case is to understate the matter. That is not to say that it was inevitable that he wound up behind bars, as he did, but certainly some details about his background are in order.

Born in 1962 and deserted by his mother, John had been left in the care of an alcoholic father, who had promptly given up on him and placed him in foster care when he was five. John's foster mother, Leona, who died in 2016, did her best with her unruly charge. However, ultimately she decided, with the concurrence of the Family Court authorities, that it was best if he was returned to the supervision of the New York State Division for Youth, in whose care John spent the next six years.

Nevertheless, to her great credit, Leona didn't give up on her foster son, and in 1974, when he was eleven, she agreed to give it another go with him and the authorities agreed to allow him to go back to school. That is when I met John, and how he happened to become my first student.

****

WHAT CAN I say about the two years that John was actually my student? I did my best.

Happily, he never actually "escaped" from my classroom again; however, it would be an exaggeration to say that I managed to get him under control. Unfortunately, John's obstreperous behavior, which included frequent vocal outbursts, and, occasionally, physical fights with his fellow students, certainly prevented us from making very much headway with his formal education.

At one point, in his second year with me, when John's behavior had improved somewhat, I reached into my Austinesque bag of coaching-cum-teaching tricks and decided to reward John by offering to take him on a fishing trip to a local creek in return for "giving" me a productive and non-violent week at school.

156

As an additional inducement, I offered John the chance to bring Tony, a new friend and positive role model, who had helped him overcome the stigma attached to attending resource room. Not that I had had much experience fishing before, aside from a few boat trips as a boy. I at least remembered to buy some bait first. I also was a little careless in picking the spot: the pond near the town of Westerlo that I ultimately chose for our outing was actually located on a private property, and the three of us wound up being chased off by the irate owner.

Nevertheless, the field trip with "Mr. B" as John liked to call me, was a success. John settled down, at least for a while. However, inevitably, his recalcitrant self surfaced again. Soon the pattern became all too familiar: aggressive behavior, followed by a suspension. Followed by a spurt of cooperation. Followed by more aggression, leading to another suspension. And so on. I did my best, but there was only so much I could do.

Ultimately, John wound up finishing the eighth grade on home instruction.

I was left to move on; there were other challenges to meet, other students to assist. In the end, even the most energetic and giving teacher has to make a judgment call about how many of his own finite resources he will devote to a particular student. Moreover, John was no longer my student.

One year later I was surprised if not exactly shocked to hear that my refractory young friend had started a fire in a locker at the high school.

Unsurprisingly, in 1977 I was asked to represent John at the superintendent's meeting where his fate would be decided. Unfortunately, my attendance didn't help matters very much. The result of the hearing was John's expulsion from Bethlehem. He was immediately enrolled in the La Salle School for Boys in Albany. La Salle was the type of school that used to be referred to as a reform school. John became a residential student as there were dormitories on site.

Unsurprisingly, he did not graduate. At that point we lost touch. Later, I learned that John had found work with a private building contractor. Evidently he was a gifted carpenter. Not that this wound up doing him—or society—much good.

****

I HAVE to say that I *was* shocked to learn, albeit somewhat after the fact, what happened in John's life not long after.

Flash forward twenty years, to 1999, when I was at the apex of my bifurcated career at Bethlehem, teaching special education during the day, while also coaching three sports, including the varsity baseball team—the same one which would shortly be taken away from me. One day that fraught year I was shopping at the local Radio Shack when I happened to run into Dan, John's younger foster brother and also a former student, whom I also had lost touch with.

I was pleased to see Dan, who apparently had done well for himself as the store manager. "And how is John?" I asked.

"Not so good," Dan replied.

"I might as well tell you," Dan said. "John is in jail."

That in itself didn't surprise me so much. I always knew that there was a possibility that John might go off the rails.

Pause.

"And what is he in for?" I asked hesitantly.

Pause.

"Murder. Murder in the second degree…"

And where was he?

"Sing Sing."

Sing Sing. Hearing the name of New York's most infamous prison—the same one which housed such notorious inmates as serial killers Alfred Fish and David Berkowitz, and where the last inmate sentenced to death by the state, James Gray, was electrocuted in 1962, as figured in countless Hollywood gangland movies, literally sent shivers down my spine.

Sing Sing.

Murder. Sing Sing. It was hard to get my head around.

****

SEVERAL YEARS and numerous jail visits later, after I reconnected with John, and I had the gumption to ask him about the crime, he told me what happened. He explained that he met a man, later identified as a furniture salesman, in a bar in Albany who told him that he had some drugs to sell. The two returned to the salesman's apartment to do the deal.

John waited in the living room for his "friend" to bring said drugs out. According to John, the man returned without his clothing and began to make sexual advances toward him. Feeling the need to defend himself, John picked up a hammer, which was laying nearby, and bludgeoned his would-be seducer to death.

At least that is how John told it.

Significantly, even at that point, thirteen years or so after the crime, he refused to take full responsibility for it. It was just an accident, he said.

Obviously, John's rehabilitation was still a work in progress.

****

IN THE MEANTIME, John did a favor for me and another student who I feared was also headed down the wrong road.

"Scared Straight," as some readers may recall, was the prison program inspired by the 1978 award-winning documentary film of the same name in which young criminal offenders were put together with "lifers" in order to "scare them straight," i.e., frighten them from pursuing a life of crime, lest they end up behind bars.

In early 1999, several months after I found out what happened to John and his current whereabouts, I decided to try a "Scared Straight" program of my own for a current student of mine—let's call him Peter—who I was worried about.

Like John, Peter had come from a difficult family background. While still in elementary school he had discovered his baby sister dead in her crib, apparently from Sudden Infant Death Syndrome, which had deeply affected him.

School was not a priority for Peter, to say the least. He frequently displayed a defiant attitude and was often disruptive in class. My appeals for support from his parents did not improve his school performance. I even arranged for him to play on a community basketball team and would sometimes pick him up at home and drive him to his games. On several occasions, neither parent was home when I arrived, and I saw that that Peter and his younger brother, who was also my student, had to fend for themselves for dinner.

An intervention of some kind was definitely in order. All in all, Peter seemed the right student to bring to Sing Sing to meet someone who resembled him twenty-five years before. Was John willing to participate? He was.

I admit that in assuming that John was mature enough to participate—after all I hadn't seen him in twenty years, and that was before his life took such a drastic turn—I was taking a big chance, but I felt that it was a chance worth taking. He had sounded reasonably responsible in his letters. Worse come to worse, we could always leave.

John also explained in a letter the procedure for visitors to Sing Sing. Next I contacted the father of Peter who gave his permission for the experiment. So did my department.

So off we were to Sing Sing. The question was: would it work? Would John be able to "scare" his younger incarnation straight?

The ancient correctional facility itself was uncomfortably close to the way I remembered it from 1930s movies: an aging riverside fortress ringed with concrete, razor wire, and guard towers.

The similarity became more uncomfortable and disturbing, as Peter and I passed through the entrance of one of the older structures with a "Visitors" sign on it, and were asked to produce several forms of identification, as John had earlier indicated. The guard on duty asked me how I happened to know our incarcerated host.

I told him that I used to be his teacher, to which he responded with a quizzical look. Evidently he had not heard that before. As far as Peter was concerned, I said that he was a friend.

After a thorough—and thoroughly nerve-racking—electronic identity check, followed by an intense frisking and the removal of our shoes, Peter and I proceeded through a series of electronically-bolted iron doors. The jarring noise made by each successively closing portal had a deafening finality to it.

Somewhat to my surprise, as well as Peter's, we were ushered into a large cafeteria-type room for our visit. I suppose that I had thought that we would be separated from John and would have to talk to him through a partition of some sort, perhaps via a phone, as in the movies.

Instead my increasingly anxious charge and I were told to sit at a numerically-designated table, face a certain direction, and wait for John to be "brought out" (what a horrible phrase!). Other inmates, the majority of them African-American, dressed in green prison jumpsuits, were seated at other tables, conversing with their "guests" under the watchful eyes of several less-than-genial-looking guards.

Just another day at Sing Sing Correctional Institute. I will admit that I was feeling somewhat less than relaxed.

Suddenly I espied an inmate approaching our table. He recognized me before I recognized him. It was John, of course. I suppressed a double take.

The man who stood before me looked nothing like the boy I had known twenty years before. I suppose I should have anticipated this, but I hadn't. For one thing, there was the hair. In place of the long shaggy blonde hair John the boy used to wear, John the man had but a few coils of hair on his nearly bald head. His wan face reflected the ten years he had already spent behind bars.

He still looked "tough," but it was a different kind of tough. Gone was John the miscreant student's defiant glare. In its place was the hardened appearance of a man who had become a survivor in an environment of constant danger. He had the watchful eyes of a man that was ever wary of the next imminent threat.

161

To say that John was pleased to see me is to understate the case. We were actually his first visitors since his incarceration a decade before.

"So this is Peter," he remarked. I looked over at Peter, who was absolutely petrified by this point.

Noticing this, John immediately tried to put Peter at ease, launching into a humorous conversation about having Mr. B as a teacher.

"How do you like having Mr. B. as a teacher?" John asked the young reflection of himself.

"It's OK, I guess," Peter replied haltingly.

"Have you gone on any trips with Mr. B.," he asked.

"He's taken me to some basketball games."

A moment later I brought up the purpose of this unusual field trip—to tell it like it is, i.e., to explain what life behind bars was really like. I asked John to be completely honest with Peter. Whereupon John launched into a straightforward account of his incarcerated existence, detailing what prison was really like. And so he did, calmly expatiating about everything from the everyday drudgery of his existence to the more unseemly aspects of prison life, including the violence. No details were spared. If Peter had been petrified before, now he was transmogrified.

Next I asked John to take himself back in time and trace his path from his—and my—middle school resource room to his cell in Sing Sing.

And so he did. John spoke about how he gotten mixed up with the wrong crowd in high school and the drugs he had done.

He stopped short at recounting the heinous crime he had actually committed. That would have been too much. Anyway, it wasn't necessary. I could see from Peter's countenance that our day trip to Sing Sing had been effective.

John ended his tale of woe by asking Peter to look around the room where we were seated, and especially at the faces of the other inmates. "Look into their eyes," he said. "Look at their faces. Peter, you and Mr. B. are going home now; I'm not going anywhere for a long time, possibly forever. Before you go, take a look around. This is not a place you want to be."

162

I looked over at Peter. He had gotten the message.

****

DID it take, you ask?

It did—at least I think it did.

All I can say is that somehow Peter managed to stay out of trouble. The last I checked he was gainfully employed and living with his mother in Schenectady. In light of the troubled adolescent I remembered, I considered this good news.

Did the day trip to Sing Sing help "scare him straight?"

I would like to think that it helped.

****

AND John?

John is still in jail. Since my initial visit with him nearly twenty years ago, I have visited my former student in a number of prisons, ranging from medium security to maximum, depending on how well or poorly John has been behaving lately. I know the routine now; I also have a fairly comprehensive knowledge of the New York State prison system. Realizing being granted parole is not a given in his case, John asked me to write to the Board on his behalf. I recently submitted a letter in which I highlighted his efforts with Peter, but I realize gaining his release will be an uphill battle. From a societal perspective I guess it has to be.

However, I always will be grateful for what he did with Peter.

To this day my wife Debbie and I remain John's only visitors from the outside world.

CHAPTER 9:
JESSE BALL

NO DOUBT about it: I enjoyed coaching women's softball and basketball and soccer, and all the sports—have I left out any?—I coached at Bethlehem in the 70s, 80s, and 90s. I also learned a lot from those experiences and wouldn't have traded them for anything in the world.

But, of course, my dream had *always* been to coach baseball. In fact, when I first arrived at Bethlehem in 1974, it had been the only sport I had been interested in—as well as the only one I was technically qualified to coach!

I like to think that I surprised myself. I know for sure that Joe would have been surprised to hear that I was coaching softball, which he considered a lower form of baseball. And soccer? Don't even think about it.

For Joe, really, there was only one sport. And in my heart of hearts, I had to admit, while I enjoyed the other sports, baseball was in my blood. You can therefore imagine how thrilled I was when, in 1985—a full decade after I came to Bethlehem, and after it seemed I had coached every other sport—the gods relented and I finally got the opportunity to coach the freshman baseball team.

More than just the gods were involved in my hire. I also had a few humans to thank, most notably the then-freshman baseball coach, Nelson Harrington, who had told me that he would move up to junior varsity to make room for me with the frosh. Nelson, a middle school physical education teacher, a colleague and friend, was already familiar with my baseball skills, as well as my love for the game.

164

Indeed, Nelson was so intent on seeing me succeed him as freshman coach that after the resignation of the then varsity coach made room in the Bethlehem coaching ranks, he told me he intended to resign if I didn't get the position! That's a friend!

Fortunately, as much as I appreciated it, Nelson's touching offer to commit *hara-kiri* on my behalf was not necessary, and my star-crossed career as a baseball coach at Bethlehem, one that would last another decade and a half, and ultimately culminate in controversy and personal tragedy, had begun.

Of course I didn't know that at the time.

Everything was sweetness and light as far as I was concerned. I also was grateful to Charlie Gunner, the principal at the time, and Ray Sliter for inaugurating my baseball coaching career. The sky was blue with no clouds--bureaucratic or otherwise—in sight.

And so they would remain for quite a while. In fact, looking back, one could say that the years from 1985 to 2000, which ultimately saw me rise to the position of varsity coach, before I was abruptly terminated—essentially for my love of the sport— were generally happy but for the loss of my parents.

Not that I was unduly unhappy before. However, unquestionably, there had been something missing in my life: the opportunity to coach the sport I loved.

There also had been something else missing in my life: the right partner. As fate would have it, I found her shortly after my baseball career began—and just before my father's death.

****

TO BE SURE, as prepared as I was for it—or thought I was prepared for it—the challenge of coaching freshman baseball proved more of a challenge than I expected. Or at least certain aspects of it did.

For example, the tryout. Suddenly I had to deal with seventy-two fourteen and fifteen-year-old eager beavers, all desperate for one of the fifteen or sixteen open roster spots. The exact number was usually determined by how many uniforms, or should I say normal-sized uniforms, were available: I actually had to buy

165

uniforms for two of the super-sized kids—Sean Lynch and John Reagan, each of whom, somewhat incredibly, were six feet five inches tall and weighed 240 pounds.

I had no problem with that, of course, once I finally weaned the mob-sized group of aspiring players down to a manageable number. It would have been easier, or at least slightly easier, if the weather had cooperated and I had been able to evaluate the prospects outdoors, or if Bethlehem had a normal-sized gym for conducting a proper indoor tryout.

But it was March—a very cold March, in point of fact—and Bethlehem Middle School, while blessed in other ways, had two relatively small gyms, neither of which was appropriate for an indoor baseball tryout for seventy-two adolescent candidates.

So I wound up having to try out one bunch in one gym one day, then another the next day in the second gym, for two full six-day weeks. All in all it was quite a passage. I am not going to say it was an ordeal because it did have its fun moments. However, I can authoritatively state that I never threw so many batting practice pitches or hit as many fungos.

****

IT was worth it.

My first season with the Bethlehem frosh Eagles resulted in a Suburban Council League record of 7 – 7. One of the reasons for this, I like to think, is the practice routine I developed. Every day every player would play both the infield and the outfield, as well as hit.

At the age of fourteen or fifteen, deciding on the right defensive position, in my opinion, should remain an open question pending further experience. Most kids coming out of Little League, as most of my freshman players did, rebel at the thought of playing outfield, since generally speaking, you only were sent to the outfield if you "stunk"—or at least that is the way many if not most of them remembered it. So I would leave that decision open.

166

Also, each practice would end with a fun activity such as "nickels"[8] or "the running game"[9] just the way Joe used to do. There was definitely some talent on the squad, but it also became clear to me that, especially with the weather the way it was that spring, which limited our practice time, I would not be able to do an adequate job with the kids I had, or meet everyone's expectations.

Consequently, the summer of 1985 brought the inception of the neighborhood pick-up games, as well as the philosophy and culture that came to surround it, which came to be known as "Jesse Ball." Of course, the idea of this sort of spontaneous and unencumbered school activity, which I felt and still feel should be the essence of a healthy childhood, was hardly original: like so much of what I did as a coach, it originated with Joe.

It also struck many of my suburbanite neighbors as strange. Nevertheless, even though I knew I was swimming against the tide, I was determined to realize my vision for bringing Jesse Ball—or Joe Ball, really, as it ought to have been called—to the Albany region. Every day that June of 1985, I began driving up to the middle school field with my equipment and patiently waited for potential latter-day Emeralds to show up. I barely had enough players to play a game, nevertheless I continued to show up every day promptly at noon.

My perseverance paid off: by August word of the increasingly popular pick-up games had gotten around, and, with regular attendance approaching fifteen, we could play.

And thus I managed to graft Joe's world onto mine.

****

---

[8] Nickels: an alternative to batting practice played as a game in which players hit and field but do not run or throw. The coach pitches, and the players get plenty of batting and fielding practice but rest their arms.
[9] The running game: A game played at practice in which the players do all the pitching, fielding and baserunning while the coach does the hitting. The players are able to practice defensive situations and gain baserunning experience.

IN THE INTERIM I continued to enjoy my on-campus experience coaching the freshmen Eagles.

With all the batting practice I was now getting, I also had to adjust my dress somewhat. With all the fungos I was now hitting, my left hand was blistering and bleeding. So I decided to break a lifelong habit and donned a batting glove on my bottom hand.

My second freshman team was a strong one, featuring a tight defense that included Chris Aloisi, Ryan Flynn, Albert Greenhalgh, David Sodergren, Kyle Snyder, and pitcher Alex Hackman. A powerful lefty, Alex wound up finishing the season with a 7 – 2 record with fifty-one strikeouts and only twenty walks in fifty-one innings. Righties Pat Doody and Randy Wilson filled out the rotation.

We wound up winning the Gold Division Championship with an overall record of 14 – 4. In the meantime, now that I was coaching men as well as women, I learned how challenging coaching players of my own gender can be, particularly in the discipline area. Pitcher Randy Wilson was particularly helpful in this regard. A prodigious athlete, Randy also had his share of personal problems, which sometimes tended to spill onto the field. "Trouble," most of my fellow coaches would have said. And trouble he turned out to be.

Randy showed just how much of a challenge he could be during our first home game of the season against Niskayuna. His earlier run-ins with the school authorities meant that he was not eligible for the starting lineup, though I held out the possibility of bringing him in later.

Alex Hackman, our starting pitcher, had taken a 5 – 3 lead into the seventh and final inning when he started to tire. Walking to the mound, I told my unpredictable reliever to get loose. After the first two batters reached base, I turned to see if Randy was ready.

Where was Randy? I looked around. For some reason he had left the field. I quickly apprehended why: my star reliever was kissing a girl on the hood of a nearby parked car. I still had a sense of humor about the situation. Oh yes, I may have forgotten to tell you that that is a major prerequisite for high school coaching.

"Randy," I yelled over, "when I told you to warm up, I didn't mean like that!" "Get in there," I ordered.

"Sure Coach," he said casually. Personally, I thought he was rather nonchalant about the situation, but that was Randy. Of course, it is important to remember, he *was* fifteen.

Bringing Randy in turned out to be a good move. Although he allowed one hit, which led to another run by Niskayuna, he struck the next and final batter out, preserving the win. I ran over to congratulate him on the win, but Randy was confused.

"Hey, wait," he asked, as I ushered him off the mound. "What inning is this?" That was Randy Wilson.

Although I enjoyed Randy and did my best to work with him and correct his exuberant ways, there was only so much I could do, particularly if he persisted in flaunting them in public. Later that term, another less good-humored Bethlehem coach caught Randy smoking in front of a local Friendly's ice cream parlor and decided to report him to the school authorities. I did my best to save the rambunctious youth, nevertheless the hidebound powers that be decided to suspend him and he was lost to the Eagles for the duration of the season.

Exit Randy Wilson. You win some and you lose some.

I had more success with a refractory player during the next 1987 season by the name of Richard (let's call him).

Like many gifted adolescent athletes, Richard was a young man with a temper.

One day during batting practice, while I was giving the squad a workout, Richard's volatile nature got the better of him. Disappointed with his poor performance, he suddenly decided to take out his frustration on his batting helmet, promptly whirling around with his bat and smashing his helmet to pieces.

"Right," I muttered to myself.

Nevertheless, I was not about to give up on my would-be Jimmy Piersall.[10] Using a stratagem which I learned from my special education work, I explained to the fifteen-year-old that he would earn one dollar from me every time something that upset him took place, whether it be a strikeout or a bad call, and he managed to refrain from cursing or destroying equipment.

After he had amassed $12—the price of a helmet at the time—then he could have the honor of purchasing a new helmet for the team.

And so he did. Meanwhile, the Eagles went on to win their second league championship, on and off-field tantrums and smashed helmet notwithstanding, confirming that their success—as well as my success with them—was not just a flash in the pan.

****

IN 1987, while I continued to coach frosh baseball, along with women's soccer and basketball, my fertile on-and-off coaching career took off in another direction when I agreed to form a summer team for eligible sixteen-year-olds for the New York Mickey Mantle league.

Randy Gambelunghe Sr., the man who was principally responsible for this development, was a baseball man through and through. He also was the father of three sons. A bartender at the local Italian-American Community Center, Randy had recently started a Connie Mack summer team in Bethlehem for seventeen and eighteen-year-olds who wanted to continue to play baseball after the school season ended. He did this in part so that his sons could have a venue for extending their own cowhide fetish, but also as a way of contributing to the community.

One day that spring Randy asked me whether I would be interested in following his lead by creating a Mickey Mantle affiliate for the next younger group of eager local baseball players.

---

[10] Jimmy Piersall (1929-2017) was an outfielder for the Cleveland Indians who had a history of strife on and off the field. He was the subject of the 1957 film *Fear Strikes Out*.

Admittedly, I was hesitant at first. At age thirty-six, I was still playing in the Town League, the adult baseball league sponsored by the Bethlehem Parks and Recreation Department, and did not wish to give my own playing time up. Also, I was keenly aware of the daunting fiscal and logistical challenges facing anyone who tried to set up their own summer team.

The fact is, without taking away anything from high school coaching, coaching a community-based team, is considerably, if not more demanding. Unlike his or her campus-based counterpart, a community-based, or volunteer coach has neither staff nor budget. He or she is responsible for the entire operation, including financing it.

Also, as I already knew, and was about to relearn, a community-based coach must deal directly with parents without the buffer of a school administration.

Still, Randy, who was familiar with my history, as well as my prolific afterschool activities, including my Jesse Ball pick-up games, was persistent, and, I have to admit, I was intrigued. For one, there was a conspicuous lack of an organized program for sixteen year olds, a difficult time for a boy with potential not to be able to hone his skills.

Secondly, starting my own Mickey Mantle team would help me bolster my relationship with the boys on the freshmen team who chose to join—although of course I never pressured any of them to do so, and in fact most of the team was comprised of boys from either the Bethlehem JV squad or from private schools.

Of course, this meant sharing my summer with another group of baseball-mad kids, but so what? Come to think of it, I was pretty mad about the game, too, was I not?

And so the next year I also began coaching Mickey Mantle.

****

AS expected, the process of financing the volunteer team was arduous, but I was able to overcome that challenge by establishing a fundraising plan with the much-appreciated assistance of team parent Mary Snyder. It was Mary's idea to send a short letter to every business in town requesting a donation of ten dollars.

The response was mixed—some businesses sent the requested amount, a few sent more; quite a few didn't send anything at all. In addition I applied for and received a $500 grant from Bethlehem Opportunities Unlimited, an organization dedicated to preventing substance abuse by providing young people with constructive activities. I also asked the family of each player if they could pay a registration fee of thirty-five dollars. They could. And so we locked up our financing.

As I expected, dealing with parents proved more difficult. In one memorable case the father of a freshman player who had had a strong season sent me a glowing letter of appreciation at season's end. The following year, when I coached the same boy in Mickey Mantle, he did not fare as well. Surprise: my erstwhile fan, the father, volubly blamed me.

The most egregious example of an obstreperous parent situation took place several years later in the 1990s. At the time one family had three boys who played Jesse Ball every day for three consecutive summers. At the end of one summer the boys' mother sent me a moving letter thanking me for my efforts in organizing these Austinesque pick-up games.

By this time I was the varsity Bethlehem coach, so my first encounter with a player in organized baseball was now at the Mickey Mantle level. As a coach I try to be careful not to place a younger player on an "older" team unless I am sure that he will get substantial playing time. I was not sure about this regarding the eldest of the three boys, so I told the youngster that I thought it would be best for him to wait to play on the Mickey Mantle team the following summer.

Several days later I received a scathing, six-page, single-spaced letter from the boys' parents severely criticizing both my evaluation of their son's abilities, as well as virtually every aspect of my coaching.

It gets better. A year later, following a school season in which I played the same boy every inning of every varsity game, I received another three-page letter from the same parents in which they blamed their son's batting slump on the fact that I had played him at second base instead of his preferred position of shortstop.

It gets better. Several years later, I learned that when the brother of the above boy was in college and he was not selected for his school's baseball team, his combative parents tried to get the coach fired, even going so far as to contact the NCAA (National Collegiate Athletic Association) to do so.

So I need not have taken it personally. I didn't—generally.

I should stress that I enjoyed and continue to enjoy working with most of the parents of "my kids," many of whom have gone on to become personal friends. Only a few create havoc.

But boy, can they sometimes create havoc.

Although it was much less common, the parents of some of my women players were also capable of giving me agitation. One such parent from my second women's softball team in 1978 vividly comes to mind in this respect. In this instance, the parent, who also happened to be a coach himself, had a habit of publicly coaching his daughter from the sidelines during our games.

Once, while I was giving the player a quick instruction from the third base coach's box before she came to the plate, she was distracted by advice from her officious father that happened to conflict with mine. "You have one coach," I yelled, "and it's me."

Joe may not have approved of softball, but I think he would have approved.

In any event, that was the last time I had a problem with that parent.

****

CHOOSING the roster for my Mickey Mantle teams posed its own set of challenges. As freshman coach, I did not hold a formal tryout because generally I had already coached more than half the Mantle players for an entire season. The problem was that the neighboring Ravena-Coeymans-Selkirk School District was also part of our Mantle team's territory.

173

Additionally, there were the players who attended private schools. Those players also had to be evaluated individually. One from that contingent actually went on to play professional baseball, and another could have, but he decided to attend the United States Military Academy at West Point instead.

Also, of course, by taking on the additional responsibility of organizing and coaching Mickey Mantle, this meant that I wound up giving even more of my summer to baseball. It also meant that between my own games in the adult Town League, nary a summer's day was without a baseball game.

Of course, too by this time, I had a partner, Debbie, who not only didn't mind all the additional coaching I was doing, but often as not was there to cheer me and the boys—or the girls—on from the sideline.

In any event, thanks in no small part to Debbie's support, things really came together for my wraparound baseball coaching career over the next ten years.

On the one hand, my freshman team, the Eagles, continued to be very successful. The combination of their innate talent and drive along with my intense Austinesque-style practices consistently helped put runs on the board. With Joe looking over my shoulder, I made sure that every player mastered the art of bunting and learned the fundamentals of fielding, throwing, hitting, and base running. With the pitching staff I worked on proper mechanics, control, changing speeds, the curve ball, how to increase velocity, pick-offs, and fielding the position in that order.

No baseball team can succeed without a skilled catcher, and I worked hard with our freshman catchers to help them receive well, block pitches in the dirt, develop efficient footwork, throw quickly, and call a game. Last but not least, I made sure that all of my teams played together *as a team*, and, not so coincidentally, had fun doing it. After all, as I kept reminding my players—as well as myself when I got carried away, as I occasionally was wont to do—at the end of the day baseball *is* only a game, and if I needed anyone to help remind me of that I had Debbie.

WHICH brings me back to Debbie. When I—finally—met my future second wife and partner I was thirty-five and she was thirty-four. To say that I was ready for a new partner is to understate the case. I am not sure you can say that I was desperate, but after six years of singlehood I certainly felt the lack of a companion and partner. At the same time, I didn't feel like waiting for a chance encounter at a disco—not that I frequented discos very much anymore--or the local supermarket to find her. Now, more than five years since my breakup with Anna, I had learned to manage for myself well enough. I even had learned to cook (sort of). Still, as they say, it was time to find *her*, wherever she was. To expedite the process I decided to join a local, nonprofit matchmaking group with the quaint name of the Common Interest Group, sort of a prehistoric version of Match.com.

And, looking back, quaint it was. Upon signing up, each new member was asked to fill out a personal profile that included basic personal information, age, height, and weight, along with interests and habits. The cooperating members' responses were then collated on two grids—yes, you read that right, grids—one for women, another for men. If a member's profile interested you, you would then write a letter—yes, a letter, remember letters?—care of the group. This is how things were done in the pre-Internet days, and this is how Debbie and I met. True story.

Did we click? Yes—and in more ways than one. As a special education teacher I was particularly drawn to Debbie because of her work as a child protective caseworker. Indeed I was in awe of her because of what she did. Being charged with protecting a child in a volatile domestic situation, as she was, or making the decision to remove a child who she deemed to be in imminent risk, as she often did, entailed considerable stress, to say the least, and to a greater degree than my taxing teaching job did, I should say.

Happily, we also clicked as a couple on the other requisite levels. Within a few weeks of our first meeting we were off to the races, as they say, and, I am pleased to say, we haven't looked back since. Quaint though it was, the Common Interest Group worked for us.

Fortunately, too, Debbie and my common interests also extended to sports, at least to a degree. It would be an exaggeration to say that Debbie was as addicted to the game— including watching it. *Is* there anyone as addicted to baseball as I am? I am not sure. Both then and today, even with all the teaching, coaching, and playing activities on my plate, I still manage to catch several televised games a week.

But Debbie enjoyed the game, and just as importantly, she understood it, including the underlying psychological dynamics of the sport—sometimes even in a way which I didn't, allowing me to see *and* appreciate the game and the players, including *my* players, in a more holistic way, as it were, as three dimensional human beings, and not *just* athletes.

Unlike Anna—If I can compare the two, bearing in mind that my first wife was ten years younger than Deb (as was I at the time)—Debbie understood my passion for and drive to coach. She also understood—and understands—that fulfilling that passion comes with a price. The late dinners, the postponed vacations, the loss of personal time, the extended time apart— she readily came to understand and accept these as part of the job description of being the partner and wife of Coach Can Do.

She even became a Yankee fan to boot! Thank you Common Interest Group!

****

AS it happens, I met Debbie shortly before a great personal tragedy.

In October, 1986, shortly after we met, I went home to Jamaica over Columbus Day weekend to visit with my parents as had become my habit during the post-Anna era.

Little did I know that this would be the last ever weekend I would spend with the two of them.

176

Looking back, this visit, like most of my visits back to Jamaica, is basically a blur of seeing friends, enjoying my mother's home cooking, and watching sports on TV with my father. My most vivid recollection was joining Harry as he watched the New York Giants play football on TV, as the quarterback, Fran Tarkenton, took off on one of his patented scrambles and magically evaded the opposing behemoths (I forget who the Giants were playing), Houdini-like, as they dove in vain to catch him, and hearing my father's uproarious laugh as my mother puttered away in the kitchen.

And then I was off for the Port Authority Bus Terminal for the bus to Albany, where I looked forward to spending the remainder of the weekend with my new prospective partner, Debbie.

Although Harry, now retired, was now in his seventies and had had a history of heart problems, I was not particularly worried about him. Perhaps, in hindsight, I ought to have been. As far as I knew he still had plenty of time left on his parking ticket on Earth.

Unfortunately, he didn't...

The following day, after Debbie had helped me with my grocery shopping for the rest of the week, I returned to my apartment to find a note from the Bethlehem Police Department asking me to call them, which I did immediately, whereupon I was informed that my mother was trying to reach me.

An anxious moment later I was on the phone with my mother.
"Hi. Mom," I said. "What's up?"
Beat.
The rest of the exchange went something like this:
"Dad died last night."
"What? How can that be? He was fine when I left."
"He had a massive heart attack. I found him on the floor..."
Fade to black...

****

AND things stayed black, pretty much, that fall.

My father, my lodestar, gone. There are no words, really, for the darkness I felt.

Fortunately, I had Debbie. If anything her comfort and companionship during my immediate -mourning period and beyond helped cement our relationship.

So yes, I had Debbie.

And of course I had my teaching.

And of course I had my coaching.

..And my coaching.

...And my coaching.

****

MY father wouldn't have had it any other way.

The next year, 1987, was something of a transitional year for me and my hydra-headed coaching career for understandable reasons.

However, by the following year, 1988, thanks in no small part to Debbie's stalwart support, I had hit my stride again—and so had my cherished Mickey Mantle team.

One game that season stands out for me. Our opponent was the formidable Latham Shakers from North Colonie.

In the third inning, with the score tied 1 – 1, something happened in that game I had never seen before and haven't seen since. After a lead-off walk, I decided to call for a sacrifice bunt to move the runner, John Hoffman, into scoring position. Second baseman Craig Weinert laid down a perfect bunt that the Latham third baseman could only pray would roll foul.

It didn't. Both Hoffman and Weinert were now safe.

Next up was shortstop David Sodergren. I thought it worked once; why not twice? Sodergren expertly bunted the ball up the first baseline. The Latham first baseman charged, fielded, and turned to throw to first. However, the second baseman had been trying to keep the lead runner close and was late covering first. Consequently, his throw sailed down the right field line, allowing both Hoffman and Weinert to score.

In the end, we wound up bunting five consecutive batters before Latham recorded a single out. The five consecutive bunts led to an eight-run inning which broke the game wide open. The rest of the season went like that. Ultimately my Mickey Mantle team wound up with an impressive 19 – 7 record and a New York State championship.

At our end-of-season party, the team presented me with a team shirt, which had been adapted from a T-shirt for Nancy Reagan's anti-drug campaign, with the words JUST SAY NO on the back.

The front had one word: BUNTING. As they say, you had to have been there.

The 1989 Mickey Mantle team was notable for the appearance of three players who went on to bigger and better things: Mark Houston, Cameron Smith, and Matt Quatraro. Houston, who attended the private Albany Academy, was a triple threat, ably filling the bill as pitcher, hitter, and shortstop. He would go on to enjoy an exceptional athletic career at West Point, where he played for both the Black Knights baseball and football teams, before entering military service, reaching the rank of colonel (I believe).

Ultimately, Mark wound up as chairman of the Military Science Department at the University of Virginia.

Cameron Smith, a versatile player from Ravena-Coeymanns-Selkirk High School, also made his debut at age fifteen. Cameron could catch and play third base and/or the outfield. However his impressive arm strength persuaded me that his potential would best be utilized as a pitcher.

My intuition—along with my original decision to pick him—proved on the money. Cameron, who went on to play for the Ithaca College varsity, wound up being drafted by the Detroit Tigers. He would go on to have a reasonably successful minor league career as a pitcher, reaching the AAA level with three different organizations.

And then there was Matt. I first met Matt when he began playing Jesse Ball at the age of 11. A lanky adolescent who

179

quickly stood out for his electric bat speed, he made the game look easy.

I am sure that I am biased, but he reminded me of that old quote about Joe DiMaggio: "You never saw him sweat." It's a cliché but the ball literally exploded off his bat. Matt was the reason Debbie decided to make my Christmas gift that year a protective "L-screen" in order to protect me for when I threw my prodigy batting practice.

Ultimately, Matt, who graduated from BCHS in 1992, after playing for both my freshman and Mickey Mantle teams, would make All American at Old Dominion University in Virginia where he was drafted by the Tampa Bay Rays. He went on to have a successful nine-year career at the minor league level, amassing a respectable composite batting average of .286. After a nine-year minor league coaching and managing career with Tampa, Matt would ultimately reach baseball's pinnacle, the major leagues, in 2013 when he was hired as the Assistant Hitting Coach for the formidable Cleveland Indians.

In any event, the 1989 Mickey Mantle season was an outstanding one, and we wound up achieving a record of 16 – 6. In 1990, with our three best players a year older, we steamrollered the competition. Debbie, who by now had become a welcome fixture at the summer games, asked me, "Are you that good or are they"—meaning our opponents—"that bad?"

Well, I have to say unashamedly, we were *that* good, and that year we made it all the way to the Mickey Mantle World Series, finishing the season 29 – 5. We would continue to be successful, compiling a combined 83 – 33 record from 1991-1995, when my star-crossed career as varsity baseball coach began.

And somewhere up there I knew my father was smiling down on me.

CHAPTER 10:
THE POISONED CHALICE
(OR THE LONG TUNNEL)

WEBSTER'S defines *poisoned chalice* as "something which is initially regarded as advantageous, but which is later recognized to be disadvantageous or harmful, and bringing about the downfall of its recipient."

That essentially describes the excruciating experience I had beginning in 1994, when I formally applied for the position of head baseball coach at Bethlehem Central High School and which culminated with my dismissal and personal tragedy.

In the event, it took six long years, and two battles—one of which I won, the second of which I lost—for the poison to take full effect.

****

TO BE SURE, poison and tragedy were the furthest things from my mind in the fall of 1994 when I applied to head the baseball program at BCHS.

Oddly enough, the first I heard that the position was open, or would soon be open, was at the Mickey Mantle postseason picnic in August, 1994 when one of the players' parents mentioned that Ken Hodge, the long-time head coach, was resigning to become assistant baseball coach at the College of Saint Rose, a small, if well-regarded private college in Albany. After spending most of his career on the high school baseball diamond, Ken had decided to "move up" to the college level, even if this entailed taking a subordinate spot on the Saint Rose team. Nothing so strange

181

about that. I wished nothing for the best for Ken, with whom I had worked closely over the years.

What *was* strange, I thought, was that no one in the Bethlehem administration had bothered to inform me of the opening. I attributed this failure to a bureaucratic oversight. Little did I suspect that the powers that be had already decided to choose someone else for the position.

Oh well, I thought, things happen.

Soon stranger—and more unsettling—things began to happen.

I should insert here that between my on-campus position as freshman baseball coach, and my off-campus work with my Mickey Mantle team and running the neighborhood "Jesse Ball" games, as well as the numerous women's sports teams I continued to coach, I was certainly fulfilled as both a sports coach and a baseball coach, indeed more than fulfilled.

Still, for twenty years, ever since I first started teaching at Bethlehem all the way back in 1974 and asked then athletic director Ray Sliter about whether he needed a baseball coach, my ultimate dream had been to be head baseball coach, as it would be for any high school coach worth his salt. And how could it not?

Granted, I didn't think about it very much, or allow myself to think about it, but the idea of heading a program for my first love, baseball, had always been there. Now, suddenly, with Ken's imminent departure, that vivid, if dormant dream was about to be realized.

Or so I thought.

Although I didn't presume that the head coach position *would* be offered to me, if and when it became available, which had certainly not been a given in light of the fact that Ken had been coach for nine years and was still in his 50s, I thought that I would have a very good chance of being promoted to head, if and when Ken ever departed the Bethlehem dugout.

I *certainly* thought that if and when the head coach position became available, that I would have a fair shake at getting it, especially after having been chosen to be head coach of the

Adirondack Region baseball team for the Empire State Games earlier that year.

I *absolutely* did *not* expect to have to *fight* to get a fair shake at getting the position, no less that having secured and won the coveted and contested position that it would ultimately be wrested from me because of my love of coaching!

But that, in a nutshell, is what took place over the next six years.

****

A FEW further words of preface here, if I may.

Mind, the whole long sordid story of how I fought for, and won, but ultimately lost the six-year-long fight to be head baseball coach at Bethlehem, with all of its twists and turns, would fill a separate book. Indeed, my first effort to do just that nearly *did* fill a separate book.

That, I daresay, is not the book you, reader, want to read, nor the one I wish to write *now*.

No, you want to read about my remarkable—if not miraculous—comeback, and remarkable, if not miraculous it was.

Fair enough. But first you need to know what I came back *from*.

And I came back from a lot, as the truncated version of my ordeal that follows will demonstrate.

And yes, there is some good stuff in there, too, including several of the greatest games I ever coached, and a banquet that moved me to tears. *Keep reading!*

Still, looking back at the six-year period extending from the end of 1994 to the end of 2000, it all seems like one long tunnel, punctuated by occasional shafts of light.

The moral of the story, or at least this part of the story?

There is none, really, except that sometimes bad things happen to good people.

And that bureaucrats, like bees, are basically the same everywhere.

****

183

IN MY CASE, it turns out, there was a whole nest of bureaucrats embedded in the walls of Bethlehem Central High School. And they definitely didn't like me.

I should add that until this point my relations with said bureaucrats, i.e., the Bethlehem administration, including both the superintendent and the athletic director, each of whom would play featured roles in the double-header melodrama to come, had been amicable, if perfunctory.

There certainly had been nothing in my relations with either to suggest otherwise. The first indication that perhaps this was not the case came in late October, 1994, two months after I had formally applied for the top baseball position, in the form of an article in *The Spotlight*, the local weekly town newspaper, announcing Ken Hodge's pending departure as head coach. "Probable Departure of Hodge Signals End of an Era," read the headline.

And with a 156 – 74 win-loss record, including three sectional championships (1990, 1992, and 1993) a memorable era it was. And *Mazel Tov* to Ken.

"Hodge leaves behind a Bethlehem baseball program to the rebuilding stages to confirmed replacement coach John Furey and freshman coach Jesse Braverman," the upbeat article noted.

"Confirmed?"

By whom?

"Jess," Deb said after I gave her the suspicious article to read. "There's something wrong."

There certainly seemed to be.

I should say at this point I still had faith in the System, insofar as the powers that ruled both the Bethlehem school district and Bethlehem High School could be called a system.

I should also add that I had nothing against John Furey, the putative "replacement coach," with whom I was friendly.

However, I don't think I am being biased when I say my accomplishments, experience, and dedication made me a deserving candidate.

But of course that isn't really the point. The point is that I wasn't given a fair shake.

****

I FOUND OUT just how wrong—dare I say rotten?—things were in the state of Bethlehem (so to speak) a month later, in November, 1994 when, after an oddly cursory interview with the above athletic director, *and* after learning that John Furey had indeed been chosen for the position—I am foreshortening here—I *also* found out that the director had *not* contacted *any* of the three coaches who I had listed as references in my application.

Why? I don't have the definitive answer to that question. I can't say that I ever will, anymore than Joseph K., the "hero" of *The Trial*, knew what crime he had committed when Willem and Franz, the officers of the nameless state K. had offended, came to arrest him.

Somehow, in some way I had offended the Bethlehem powers that be—at least to the point where they were willing to deny me due process.

I would go on to offend them some more.

Not that that was my intention—at least at that point.

All I knew at that point of this Kafkaesque tale was that I had been robbed.

I also knew that I had to fight this gross injustice. Joe would have insisted.

Every fiber of my being did. I should hasten to state that I am not a pugilist by nature. Indeed, I can count the number of times I have "lost it" on the fingers of one hand.

Moreover, I can assure you, all such rare occurrences took place well away from the school premises, and were related to calls or decisions by umpires or referees I may or may not have cared for. I may not be Eddie Stanky, but I am no milquetoast.

However, at least until that point, as far as the Bethlehem administration was concerned, I had basically been the Good Soldier Schweik. I certainly was no protester. As we have seen, throughout my high school and college years, which coincided with the anti-Vietnam War and Student Power movements, as much as I may have sympathized with the student protesters, I had stood aside.

I certainly had no issue with Authority, per se, either in the abstract or the concrete.

Now, to my distress and surprise, I did.

Indeed you could say that my whole conception of Authority, or Power, was about to change, as well as the occasional need to fight it.

And so, reluctantly, I decided to "fight the powers that be," in the memorable words of the Public Enemy song that was blasting out of car radios that year.

And a long, and ultimately futile fight it turned out to be, even if I did win the first engagement.

****

THE climax of the first battle of the war took place several agonistic weeks later at the regular monthly scheduled meeting of the Bethlehem Central District School Board.

To be sure, there was nothing regular about this meeting of the school board. The agendas for these meetings were usually somewhat lengthy and dealt with a long list of budgetary and curricular affairs matters and the like. Occasionally disagreements occurred, as they do at most school board meetings, but rarely was there any drama.

This meeting promised to be different. There was only one item on the agenda that night: to discuss the superintendent's recommendation to hire John Furey for the position of head coach of the Bethlehem High Varsity Baseball Team, and to endorse it, or, as I had petitioned the board, to give me the position. Scheduled to be present were the superintendent himself, along with the seven members of the board. The event, which took place at the board's small building on Adams Place, was open to the public. Afterward, the board would take a vote to endorse the superintendent's recommendation—or overturn it.

I should reiterate that up until the tempestuous events leading up to that evening—which also included a flood of calls and letters from the community protesting the original decision to hire Furey and a second, palpably fairer, interview for the position for which my references *were* actually called, leading nevertheless to the same frustrating result, before my final appeal to the board—that my relations with the superintendent had by and large been friendly, if somewhat superficial.

Although it would be an exaggeration to say that the senior educator was my friend, I certainly respected him and had every reason to believe he did me, as both a teacher and coach. He had arrived in Bethlehem six years before with a formidable educational resume, and as far as I could judge, he had certainly lived up to his billing. I remember being impressed with the eloquent address he delivered to the entire district staff on the first day of school every September.

The superintendent struck me as having a coherent vision for Bethlehem Central and skillfully motivating the nine hundred and fifty-large teaching and non-instructional staff to fulfill it. The occasional interactions I had had with him, included notifying and commending me for letters of appreciation he had received for my teaching, had been positive and encouraging. Additionally, he had been an enthusiastic supporter of a mentoring program I had initiated in which I matched former, successful special needs students with current ones who were struggling. He even asked me to write an article about the subject of mentoring in *Bethlehem Central Highlights,* the public relations bulletin of the district. I would have ventured to say that he liked and respected me.

Perhaps not.

In any event, there would be little doubt where either he or the Bethlehem athletic director stood after that intense and fateful meeting in December 1994.

****

I HAVE IT on good authority that the public meeting of the Bethlehem School Board was intense. That's because I wasn't present, or, rather, because I chose not to be present.

I *did* attend an executive session of the board prior to the public one. At that meeting, I emphasized my respect for both the superintendent and John, before recounting what I felt were my substantive qualifications for the varsity position. I was acquainted or friendly with several of the board members, and the meeting seemed to go well, insofar as I could tell in my state.

And I was in a state. How could I not be? I had pressed forward with my appeal, without really thinking about the ramifications of such a radical act, the first in the normally quiescent district's history. Now, as I sat there before this pedagogical tribunal—a new experience for me—I did reflect. It all had happened so fast. Now, I realized that I could not continue to teach at Bethlehem if my appeal failed. This was it.

I also realized that even if I won, my life as a teacher and coach, as well as a member of this small suburban community, would probably never be the same. John Furey's friends, of whom there were many, would make sure of that.

The interview was only thirty minutes, to be followed by an equally brief one with John. Then came the main event, the public meeting.

Although I was invited to the meeting, there was no way, I knew, that I could attend. So Debbie went. She could tell me how things went afterward.

Instead, I stayed at home and watched an old science fiction movie, *The Philadelphia Experiment*, set during the 1941 attack on Pearl Harbor. Written by Rod Serling, the creator of the *Twilight Zone*, the movie revolved around the theme of time travel. Today, more than twenty years later, I remember every scene.

It was a very good movie.

My mind really wasn't on the movie, of course.

****

WELL, to make a long story short, things went well that turbulent evening—or as well as I could have hoped.

A friend who was at the meeting recalls, "The room was packed, standing room only. I have no doubt that this was the best-attended school board meeting in Bethlehem history. People were lined up against the back wall. Some were standing in the doorway. I would say that there were at least 150 parents and other interested observers there."

"And then, most movingly, the parents started speaking. A lot of parents spoke—at least a dozen, I think. It was very emotional. A number of parents of both boys and girls who had played on one of Jesse's teams spoke. Most moving were the parents of Jesse's special needs students who spoke up. Some of them were so overcome with emotion that they had difficulty speaking."

"One by one they stood up and said their piece, earnestly, respectfully," the friend adds. "It reminded me a little of that painting by Norman Rockwell, the *Four Freedoms*.

"You could tell that all those testimonies and that emotion were having an effect. Jesse's wife didn't speak. That wouldn't have been in her nature. But everyone knew that she was there. Just the fact that she *was* there, bearing witness for Jesse, was enough. In a way, we were all there to bear witness, but *active witness*. And we did.

"Several of John's friends were also there, and they also spoke up in his defense, although they were in a difficult position, defending an indefensible process. The room was with Jesse. And you could tell from their faces, or most of their faces, that the board was with Jesse, too. One of the members, I forget who, was so moved by this outpouring of support that he suggested that the town have a 'Jesse Braverman Day.'

"I also remember that the Albany County Executive, Michael Breslin, was there. He had thought it important enough to attend. I was impressed by that. I was even more impressed when he questioned the superintendent about the original selection process. I thought that was a good sign."

It was.

189

Finally, around 10 p.m., after about two hours, the vote was taken. One by one the members said "yea"—to overturn the superintendent's recommendation—or "nay," to let it stand.

The result: six "yeas," one "nay."

As one can imagine Debbie left the building in shock—happy shock. Her immediate thought, of course, was to call me. But how? She didn't have a cell phone. This was still 1994, pre-connectivity days. Most people didn't have cell phones.

Fortunately someone did. He gave Debbie the phone. Debbie called me.

"You won," she breathed. "You won."

Yes, I had.

Of course I was pleased—thrilled—but the next day I wondered, what had I won?

Put another way, how poisonous would this coveted chalice be?

I was particularly bothered by a remark of a teacher friend who was in attendance that night, who happened to be watching the superintendent's face after the climactic vote, and was also close enough to hear him speak.

According to him, the superintendent's face flushed red after the vote overturning his recommendation to hire John Furey and appoint me instead was announced. Then he reportedly said, to no one in particular, "This will not stand."

He was right.

Ultimately, the board's decision did *not* stand, and I would be robbed of the Head Coach position—*again*.

****

OF COURSE, I didn't know that at the time.

All I knew is that I had won my dream job.

Of course I was happy about that. How could I not be? I had reached the mountaintop of the coaching profession. Finally I had my own baseball team.

Imagine that!

At the same time, I was also distressed by the manner with which I had won the job—the fact that I had had to fight for it, as well as the collateral damage that fight had caused, including my now terminated friendship with John Furey, and the enmity of *his* friends.

When all is said and done, Bethlehem, New York *is* a small town.

Additionally, I was concerned about my future relationship with the school administration. Toward that end, I wrote a conciliatory letter to the superintendent and the athletic director, hoping to smooth things over.

Then, well, I got on with the challenge of forging the Eagles into a winning team—again.

****

OF COURSE, any coach's first season at the varsity level would be a challenge. However, the 1995 Bethlehem team I inherited from Ken Hodge certainly had its work cut out for it. Although the Eagles had been sectional champs three times in the early 90s, the school's baseball program had suffered at all three levels the previous year.

The key player, I knew, would be pitcher-centerfielder Nate Kosoc, who was coming back from arm trouble. Would he be able to carry us, I wondered?

Eager to prepare for the challenge of leading the Eagles into battle, I hit the books over the winter, researching how best to organize an indoor practice. I found the perfect resource for the subject in a book, *Maximizing Baseball Practice,* by John Winkin, the legendary head coach at the University of Maine who led his Black Bears baseball team to six College World Series berths during an eleven-year span in the 1990s and 2000s. I figured that no one would know more about the art and science of planning effective indoor practices than an experienced baseball coach from Maine, where they have a lot of rainy days, or so I heard.

To say that I was nervous for my first game, against Burnt Hills Ballston Lake, is to understate the matter. I was only partly consoled by the knowledge that the opposing coach, Norm Hayner, was also a rookie.

Burnt Hills held us close. Still, we managed to scratch out three runs and Nate came through for us, recording eighteen of the game's outs by strikeouts. Final score: Eagles 3, Burnt Hills 0.

As far as my coaching that day, my most vivid recollection of my debut consists of basically shouting "Way to go, Nate!"

And Nate *kept* on going. By the end of the season, in May, Kosoc's record was an impressive 9 – 1 with an ERA of 0.94. Over the course of sixty-nine innings, our fireballer allowed a mere thirty-three hits, while striking out 121 and surrendering but a dozen walks. Way to go Nate!

Despite the intense pressure I was under, the Eagles wound up with a league record of 8 – 7 against an overall one of 11 – 13. Certainly nothing to be ashamed of.

Most importantly, I now knew how to do the job.

Or at least I thought I did.

And I had earned the loyalty and respect of my players, or at least I thought I did. However, it was not until an unscheduled lecture to the team on the school bus the following year that I could say that for a fact.

Although I had picked up troubling signs of varying sorts from my superiors in the district and school administration, I wasn't worried about my job security, at least just yet. I just wanted to do the best job I could.

And I did. And for the most part, I enjoyed it.

****

MY SECOND SEASON as varsity coach the following year, 1996, began on an uncertain note. The graduation of our star, Nate, left us with a pitching staff with only two varsity non-league victories to its credit.

Nevertheless, ever the optimist, I pressed on.

As it happened, we wound up losing our first three games.

Time to mix it up. At practice after the Eagles' third loss I told the team that I was going to bring some of our talented

192

sophomores into the line, whereupon some of the seniors spoke up in protest, declaring that "we had paid our dues" and so forth.

Time to read the riot act.

"OK, let's put it to a vote," I said. "Would you guys like to make the lineup based on performance or your birth certificate?"

That seemed to settle things down, at least for the moment, and, with the aid of the younger players I had brought in, we managed to win several more victories and even our record. All was well until an embarrassing, error-filled 17 – 6 rout at Shenendehowa which re-emboldened those seniors who were now sitting on the bench to rise up in protest.

The following day the cantankerous team was sharing the bus with the women's softball team en route to a game with the Shaker Blue Bison when I asked our driver to drop off the girls first so I could read them the riot act, or the high school version of it.

"At the start of the season I met with each of you guys privately to describe your projected role on the team," I said, standing up in the aisle, as the boys, not used to being lectured to, listened intently. "I also reminded you that your role was subject to change based on performance and other unforeseen circumstances, did I not?"

"Each of you accepted this, did you not?" I continued with uncharacteristic heat, not waiting for a reply to my stern query.

"Either we get off this bus as a united team," I warned, "or I will you call you a taxi and you can go home *now*."

Silence. No one volunteered to take a cab. Taking my seat, I told the driver to move on.

My impromptu talk turned out to be a turning point, both for the team, and for me.

Later that day we beat Shaker 11 – 8.

Our newly revivified team went on to win eight of our last ten games to win the Gold Division and my second season as varsity coach came to a successful end, having put the Eagles on the winning path again.

So far so good. Although I continued to experience some bad vibes from the athletic director, (who may or not still have been holding a grudge against me), as well as the occasional surly look, I had nailed down the job.

Or so I thought.

****

Meanwhile, I continued to enjoy my off-season work with my Mickey Mantle team. With two future professional players, pitcher Matt Elfeldt and catcher Dan Conway, talent on that summer's team, which included a number of current and future varsity players, abounded. Other multi-talented players on that team included centerfielder Cory Czajka, shortstop Geoff Hunter and pitcher-third baseman Pat Hughes. I could go on.

That summer also witnessed one of the greatest games I ever coached during the second round of the North Atlantic Regional Tournament. Our opponent was General Die from Baltimore, the defending National champion (the team took its name from its sponsor). Armed with an operating budget of $45,000 and a coaching staff led by the batting practice pitcher for the Orioles, this redoubtable, if not invincible foe brought an astounding 69 – 0 record into the highly anticipated game.

Perfect record or no, our opponents quickly realized that we were no pushovers. The game evolved into an epic seesaw contest, with the lead changing every inning. However it was not until we went ahead in the sixth inning, 9 to 8, that the coach of this opposing powerhouse team took us seriously enough to insert his ace pitcher. This crafty but hard-throwing lefty managed to shut down our rally, and we took a precarious one run cushion into General Die's final at bat.

The tension in the July air was literally suffocating as the undefeated home team took the plate. Standing near the dugout, my assistant coach, John Tulloch, was impressed with my calm mien. I assured him that appearances were deceiving.

"Are you kidding?" I snapped, "my heart is beating out of my chest!"

General Die was sending up its number 8, 9, and 1 hitters, in that order. The first batter was retired on a routine ground ball.

To my dismay, the next batter proceeded to place a perfect bunt single down the third base line, beating third baseman Pat Hughes's throw to first base. I pinched myself for not having Pat play in. Bunting, after all, was my forte.

Oh well, no one is perfect.

Now we had to face the top of order with the tying run aboard. *Drat!*

Thus far Die's leadoff hitter had proven to be a tough out. The count went to 1-1 after our pitcher, Travis Teeter , threw a slider for one strike followed by an inside fastball for a ball. As usual, Dan Conway had called a smart game, consistently asking for the least predictable pitch, mixing it up, just like a pro. On the next pitch, the hit and run was on with the General Die coach expecting a fastball. Instead Travis threw a slider, just off the outside corner, which the batter swung at and missed. Strike two. Now it was Dan Conway's turn to show why professional baseball was in his future, firing a strike to second base and catching the runner dead to rights. Two outs.

General Die was down to its last out. The outfield tensed up, expecting the long ball: there had been quite a few that afternoon. Instead the batter hit a simple pop out to second baseman Chris Brown.

The ensuing on-field scrum was not for a championship but for one miraculous game. Before the game no one had given us a chance. We had certainly shown them!

Anxious to share the welcome news of our victory with Deb, I ran to the back of the concession stand and dialed home (still no cell phone!). Instead of Deb I got her voice mail, so I decided to leave a message instead. "69 and 0 and is now 69 and 1," it said.

Another good omen, I thought. Perhaps '96 *would* be my year, after all.

****

IT CERTAINLY was the Yankees' year…

In October, after besting the Orioles in the American League Championship, the Yankees went against the defending champions, the Atlanta Braves, in their first World Series in fifteen years. Things got off to a less-than-promising start for the Bombers after they were trounced in the first game by a score of 12 to 1 before the shell-shocked crowd. Things looked even worse after the second game, when Bernie Williams and his fellow batsmen were again limited to one run, and the Yanks lost 4 to 1. There certainly was no joy in the Bronx—or Bronxville, for that matter, that depressing night.

However things began to turn for the Yanks in the third game, in Atlanta, when they managed to come back from a six-run deficit to win by a score of 8 to 6, the second biggest comeback in World Series history. The turning point for the game, and perhaps for the Series, may have occurred in the sixth inning, when leadoff hitter Derek Jeter hit what looked to be a routine pop up in foul territory near first base.

As infielders Fred McGriff and Mark Lemke chased the ball, Braves right fielder Jermaine Dye trotted in. The ball appeared playable by him. However, umpire Tim Welke had his back to Dye and inadvertently blocked him from getting to the ball, causing it to just drop foul. Jeter, who was on the verge of his own great run, immediately singled to start a three-run rally, capped by a Dye error in right on a Cecil Fielder single that allowed two runs to score.

The Braves never recovered from that accident, which, in retrospect, signaled the end of their great championship run of the 90s. The Yanks went on to sweep the next four games to capture their first championship since 1978 and their twenty-third overall. The Bombers' victory in the Fall Classic marked the beginning of the Yankee dynasty of the late 1990s and early 2000s. Way to go guys!

I remember watching the Yanks' ecstatic pileup after Wetteland got a despondent Lemke to foul out for the titanic last out at Yankee Stadium.

That, I thought, was another good omen.

It certainly was for the Yanks!

****

All well and good.

However, I have to append, the true emotional highlight of that championship year took place at the traditional annual banquet for the girls' basketball team when Mike Jackson, the team's long-time scorer, and my former special needs student, was honored for his lengthy service to the team, as well as to Bethlehem, with a beautifully engraved plaque. For twenty years Mike, who suffered from cerebral palsy and always wore a smile, had been the team's meticulous and unerringly accurate scorer.

However, that epochal night, of course, Mike wasn't honored for the quality of his scoring, or even his long-time service, for that matter. There were many Bethlehem staffers with twenty years or longer service who never received a plaque. The team wished to honor and reward this inspiring man for his indomitable spirit.

As Mike slowly made his way to the podium to receive his well-earned award, the entire room erupted in a deafening ovation. *Way to go Mike!*

By the time the cheers and whoops subsided, I daresay there wasn't a dry eye in the house.

Looking back on the long tunnel of the late 90s, that banquet may be the purest shaft of light.

After that, unfortunately, things got dark, very dark, again.

CHAPTER 11:
FADE TO BLACK

No one ever said life was fair, but what the Bethlehem school district did to Jesse Braverman was foul. Braverman was the head coach of the Bethlehem varsity baseball program for six years before having his successful tenure ripped out from under him.

—James Allen, *The Record*, Troy 7/10/02

TWO dates in 1997 stick out for me. The first, April 30, was the day I lost my mother. The second, September 16, was the day I began losing my job as head coach for the Eagles.

It's foolish to compare the two, and I won't. Obviously losing a parent is on another scale from losing a job. All I can say is that both events are traumatic for me, and I was emotionally unprepared for either.

Also, the first—mercifully—was not drawn out, like the second event. Taken together they made for perhaps the blackest year of my life.

I suppose I should have been more prepared for losing my mother. After all, she was eighty-three. When a parent reaches a certain age, it's only wise to prepare for the possibility and inevitability of losing her or him.

I say this in hindsight of course. Who amongst us is wise about death? Most of us live in denial of mortality, both our own and our loved ones'. So, particularly after the earlier struggles, did I.

Too, my mother could hardly be said to have been in robust health. In addition to an internist, by 1997 she was under the care of an ophthalmologist, an endocrinologist, a podiatrist, and a cardiologist. I know, because I drove her to many of her appointments. She also didn't help matters by continuing her lifelong smoking habit, an unfortunate candy store legacy.

Mentally she was very fragile. Her attention frequently wandered, and she often fell into a space somewhere between sanity and dementia where neither I nor Debbie, who helped share the burden of caring for her, could reach her.

Nevertheless, my mother was surprisingly resilient and stubborn to boot. A lot of people, including myself, expected her to fall apart after Harry died ten years before.

But she didn't.

To be sure, convincing her to sell her Jamaica home had been no easy matter. Nevertheless after myriad anxious phone calls we persuaded her to move to an apartment we found for her in 1990, and, even though neither of us really had enough time for her, and she was not the easiest person to get along with, our lives were immeasurably richer for it, and I would like to think hers was, as well.

Debbie and I saw Midge virtually every weekend and I would also visit her as often as I could during the week, though of course it was never enough, and often it was difficult to communicate with her.

But the main thing is that we were there for her, and she was there for us, as much as she could be in her diminished, if feisty way.

It would be a stretch to say that my mother was deeply involved with my life at Bethlehem, either as a teacher or a coach. If anything she was more aware of the latter. One instance that stands out is a ceremony she attended with me in 1993 at the opening day ceremonies of the Bethlehem Basketball Club, where I was asked to be a guest speaker and afterward was presented with a gorgeously engraved plaque by the Bethlehem Basketball Club in return for my service to the community. I know she appreciated that. I vividly recall seeing Midge's beaming face in the audience when I went up to accept the award from the club director.

I know she would have been horrified to learn that the service to the community for which I was honored that day ultimately proved something of a mixed blessing, and that that shiny plaque actually had an invisible serrated edge.

Fortunately she didn't live long enough to see that.

****

WEDNESDAY April 30 arrived, a pleasant upstate spring day, a good day to be alive, a good day to play baseball.

As usual, I was exhausted from the combination of my full teaching load and coaching load—bear in mind that I was still coaching both the girls' basketball team and the girls' soccer team, plus the Eagles—in addition to caring for my mother.

Nevertheless I was in a buoyant mood, and so was the team. The day before the Eagles had staged a riveting 6 – 5 comeback victory against Shenendehowa, raising our record to 7 – 3. Our scheduled opponents for that afternoon's league game were the Shaker Blue Bisons.

Tired though I was, I was looking forward to the game. As usual, my mind was already figuratively in the dugout, going over the batting order, going over how to pitch and defend the Shaker lineup, as well as pondering who should come in from the bullpen should starting pitcher Matt Tulloch need relief.

En route to the field, I had to pause momentarily on the side of the road as an ambulance sped by me in the opposite direction. You don't see ambulances every day in Bethlehem. Who was that for? I wondered for a moment before returning to my mental warm-up exercises.

When I arrived at the field one of the players told me that there was a message waiting for me at the school athletic office. My mother had fallen at the mall. It turned out that the speeding ambulance I had passed was for her. Debbie had been reached at work and was already with her in the emergency department at St. Peter's Hospital in Albany.

The doctors assured me that all was well, and my mother was resting comfortably. Debbie suggested that I go to the hospital following the game. Thankfully, the fall didn't seem to have caused serious injury. Consequently, Dr. Czajka, the father of our star centerfielder, Cory Czajka, agreed to monitor the situation by phone.

During a baseball game my focus and concentration are locked, but of course this day was different. As the game with the Blue Bison got underway, Dr.Czajka gave me the thumbs up to indicate that all was OK on the medical front. The game soon developed into a seesaw affair. In the third inning we were holding a 4 – 3 lead. Then, as the Blue Bison began mounting another threat, Dr. Czajka appeared at the front of the dugout with a concerned look and a graver message: my mother's condition had taken a turn for the worse, and I had to get to St. Peter's straightaway.

Apparently there had been an alarming drop in blood pressure, and the doctor performed emergency surgery in order to insert a pacemaker. By the time I arrived, out of breath, my mother was unconscious. Still in my baseball uniform, I along with Deb stayed by Midge's side for several hours, and with her still asleep, and with the doctors' OK, we went home for the night.

Then things took another turn for the worse…

Four long—and short—days later, Midge was gone.

Then things got shadowy again.

Now both of my parents were gone.

Somehow, with Debbie's help as well as that of my brother, Roger, with whom I remained close, I managed to get through the rest of the season and school year.

The Eagles wound up with a record of 13 – 9. To say that I took my eye off the managerial ball is to understate the case. The fact that we were able to win any games at all after that point, no less achieve a winning record, was a miracle.

****

THE GLOOM of that sad summer was broken when, in one of the milestones of my coaching career, I captained the Adirondack team to a victory and a gold medal in the Empire

State Games in front of over five thousand wildly cheering fans, the largest crowd I had ever coached before at Heritage Park.

Pandemonium broke loose on the field as the team piled on top of Ian Locke, the winning pitcher. As for me, I kneeled down in my customary spot in front of the dugout. For a brief moment, I was able to escape the abyss. Then I ran over and joined the scrum, too.

Then things went dark again.

****

THE DEMISE of my varsity baseball coaching career began on September 17, 1997, shortly after the doors of Bethlehem Central High opened for the school year and I resumed my teaching and coaching duties, when I found a letter from the athletic director in my mailbox informing me, along with the rest of the coaching staff, that the athletic directors, principals, and superintendents of the Suburban Scholastic Council, the alliance of ten (now seventeen) upstate schools to which Bethlehem belonged, had decided to reinstate the old state rule prohibiting coaches from coaching school athletes in their program regardless of level "out of season," i.e., during the summer if you were a baseball coach.

Coincidentally or not, I received the director's shocking note while I was in the midst of conducting the tryout for the following summer's Mickey Mantle team.

Did this mean that I could not go ahead with my Mickey Mantle tryout, I asked the athletic director?

Yes it did, he hastened to inform me.

Several weeks later, after a subsequent maddening round of epistolary badminton, the director confirmed that the powers that be, i.e., the Suburban League, had in their infinite wisdom, decreed that I was "in violation," whatever exactly that meant.

There is a memorable scene in *Animal House*, the classic 1978 film starring Tim Matheson and John Belushi, about the outrageous antics of Delta Tau Chi, a fraternity at Faber House, a mythical, quasi-Ivy League college in the early 1960s.

In said scene, a large college-wide meeting is held in an auditorium, where the members of the Delta Tau Chi are called to account for their manifold campus conduct violations, as well as their abysmal academic record, and Vernon Wormer, the buffoonish college dean, memorably played by character actor John Vernon, announces with relish that the entire house has been placed on something called "double secret violation."

Whatever that was. Whereupon the entire membership of the house proudly bursts into song and marches out, still unsure of what "double secret violation" actually meant.

That conveys something of how I felt after I read that memo announcing that I was "in violation."

It felt a bit like that comical-cum-Kafkaesque punishment that the powers that be had meted out to the hapless, if good-humored members of Delta Tau Chi. *In violation. Of what?*

Of course, in a way, as we know, I had been in double secret violation—or the high school variation of it--with the powers that be at my school, Bethlehem Central High School, for nearly three years, ever since I had rallied the community and forced BCHS to hire me as head coach in the first place.

And the powers that be had dropped all sorts of hints, subtle and not so, that I was in *double secret violation.*

But now I *knew* officially I was in trouble.

And there was nothing funny about it. John Belushi wasn't in the house.

On the one hand, I was surprised, as well as outraged. Although I was vaguely aware of the mysteriously reinstated rule, as well as the supposed rationale for it (which I did not necessarily disagree with)—to relieve student athletes from being under any kind of pressure to participate on their coaches' summer teams in order to improve their chances of securing a position on those same coaches' scholastic teams—the school district in effect was prohibiting me from doing something I had done for ten years.

Why now? So the new rule, or rather the Council's mysterious decision to *reinstate* a rule that it had previously discarded, was unfair in that sense.

203

For the record, for those of you are legalistically inclined, the Suburban Council coaching guidelines state that any coach of a school team in grades 9-12 in any sport, boys or girls, is prohibited from coaching an outside team in that same sport if more than 50 percent of the roster of the extra-academic team is comprised of student athletes from the school's grades 9-12 in its program.

My Mickey Mantle team rarely had varsity players on its roster, so I was not coaching the same boys who were on the school team—at least not at the same time. The summer squad was principally made up of junior varsity and freshman players. As mentioned, there were boys from the Ravena -Coeymans-Selkirk School District, as well as boys who lived in the towns of Bethlehem and Ravena, but who attended private schools.

However, since the Mickey Mantle team *was* based in Bethlehem, it would always be the case that more than 50 percent of its roster would be from Bethlehem Central. In fact, the constitution of the Eastern New York Mickey Mantle League stipulated this geographic requirement.

Put another way they had me.

So yes, I was surprised. Outraged is probably a better way of putting it. And I said so. "My coaching the Mickey Mantle team is a good thing, not a bad thing," I told the athletic director to his face. "And besides, how can you tell me what I can and cannot do when I am not at work?"

So yes, you could say that I was surprised by the administration's move.

On the other hand, I wasn't.

Even though my success with the Eagles had made me feel more secure, I knew—or a part of me had known--ever since that fateful meeting two and a half years before, where the superintendent said (or reportedly said) that "this," i.e., my hiring, would "not stand," that the powers that be would find some way to do exactly that.

Whether or not Bethlehem officials *did* in fact deliberately reinstate the rule as a means of "getting back" at me, is not for me to definitively say.

But the timing certainly seemed suspicious, to say the least.

You know what they say about paranoia. Just because you're paranoid doesn't mean that they aren't after you!

Maybe "they" were after me. Maybe "they" weren't. You tell me.

Anyway, my superiors certainly had me over the proverbial barrel. And the battle lines for the second, climactic—and, for me, tragic—war with the powers that be at Bethlehem Central High School and the Bethlehem School District, had been drawn.

Like the memo said, I was "in violation," And the fight was on.

One thing I knew for certain—and I believe the director and the superintendent also knew—was that I would *never* give up my Mickey Mantle work for the sake of staying head coach. The spirit of the late Joe Austin wouldn't have allowed it.

And Dean Wormer and his relations at Bethlehem be damned, I sure as hell wouldn't keep the matter of my putative "violation" secret.

And I didn't.

Although in the end, that didn't really matter. A poisoned chalice is a poisoned chalice.

And so the bureaucratic buzz saw which had started whirring two years before started up again.

****

AND THEN, as a result of chance meeting during an expedition to the local supermarket, it stopped, at least for a while.

At the local Grand Union supermarket in the Delaware Plaza in Delmar, I happened to run into Jim Kelly, whose son and daughter I had coached in baseball and basketball, respectively, whence I launched into my tale of woe.

Unbeknownst to me, it turned out that Jim was—and is—a crack local attorney.

"I'll take your case," he offered.

When I returned home, my ever-cheerful wife asked me whether I had gotten the groceries.

"No," I replied. "But I got an attorney."

****

PUT another way, I had lawyered up.

Now the school district and I were officially adversaries.

Whether, in light of my ultimate fate, this was a positive development is a matter of interpretation.

One thing that is clear—and was immediately clear as soon as Jim got down to the case—is that he managed to get the powers that be even madder at me than they were in the first place.

One thing that is incontestable: by using a variety of legal stratagems, Jim was able to "buy" me three more seasons as head baseball coach.

And, despite the increasingly pressurized environment in which I now had to work, I have to say, we did extraordinarily well.

With the aid of a few key players, the '98 varsity notched an 11 – 7 record in the Gold Division League, a 13 – 12 overall, and wound up losing in the Section 2 Class A New York State Sectional Championship semifinals.

Joe Austin passed away on September 8, 1998, one of the three saddest days of my life. He was 94. That year September 8 was the first day of school. I made the difficult decision to not attend his funeral in Queens so that I could be there to help my students get off to a good start. For months I struggled with guilt from this choice, until one day I had an epiphany. I realized I did not go to Joe's funeral because of what he had taught, namely that my students were counting on me in the same way I and hundreds of other kids had counted on him, so it was my duty to be there for them.

The following year the Eagles did even better, despite the sword of Damocles which was palpably hanging over me and the team, winning the championship even though we were only the No. 7 seed, culminating in an extra inning thriller in front of another massive crowd in Heritage Park, and arguably my greatest game ever—no minor claim for someone who, between

206

his various teams, had already coached approximately 1500 games—and one which I would wind up replaying in my head for some time to come, partly because it was such a remarkable contest, and partly because I was fairly sure that I would not get to repeat the experience, at least as Bethlehem head coach.

The game, against the Patriots of Schenectady High and played at Heritage Park Stadium, the minor league stadium of the Albany-Colonie Yankees, is worth recounting in detail.

"Well, we know one thing," said the opposing coach, Jerry Rosen—who, in addition to being one of the best coaches of baseball fundamentals, also happened to be a very good guy (never a given in the cutthroat world of high school baseball)— "a good guy is going to win."

I'd like to think he was right.

As far as the lineup was concerned, I thought we were in good shape with our ace, Pat Hughes. On the opposing side, Jerry Rosen had the formidable left-hander Steve Schaefer pitching for Schenectady.

My respect for Rosen and Schenectady was validated early in the game when they jumped out to a 3 – 1 lead after three unearned runs in the third inning. Clearly Pat was going to need every ounce of his competitive spirit to get us this one. And so he did—eventually.

The Eagles battled back in the fourth inning to take a 4 – 3 advantage. Pat came to bat with Ricky Long, our catcher on third with two outs. He proceeded to hit a slow roller down the third baseline and, to our bench's delight, the ill-advised off-balance throw by the Patriot third baseman to first went zooming down the right field line, allowing Ricky to score the tying run while Pat made for third.

The right fielder had retrieved the errant throw and launched the ball toward third as the airborne Pat approached. His throw also was considerably off the mark. Impulsively I urged Pat, who had just slid safely into third, to head for home. Simultaneously I saw that the Patriot left fielder had quickly retrieved the ball and was now in a position to nail Pat at the plate.

Clearly it was going to be close. It was. Fortunately the relay was slightly off, forcing the Patriot catcher, Fred Harris, to leap for the ball. At that moment the hard-charging Pat barreled into the right side of the plate with a headfirst slide which left him covered with dirt.

After the dust and personnel settled, Pat emerged, covered with dirt from head to toe, but with the go-ahead run on the scoreboard.

The game proceeded. In the top of the sixth, Schenectady pulled even when one of Pat's curves hit the dirt and bounded past our catcher, Ricky Long, on a suicide squeeze, allowing the Patriot on third base to score.

Of the hundreds of baseball games I have coached, I can't recall a situation as tense as the one which obtained in the seventh and eighth innings of that milestone game. Twice our opponents were poised to take the lead and the game, but as luck, fate, talent, and character—our talent and character I am not too immodest to say—had it, we managed to prevail.

In the top of the seventh, the Patriots had men on second and third with no outs, with their no. 3, 4, and 5 hitters on deck, but Pat, our Houdini of the mound, was able to wriggle out of his predicament with the aid of a pop-up, a strikeout, and a fly ball.

The following inning, Pat repeated his feat with the aid of no less than sixteen—you read that right, sixteen—fake pick-off throws to discourage another suicide squeeze (which he did) and a strikeout and getting the Patriots' formidable, shortstop, Josh Colafemina, to ground out.

Then it was the Eagles' turn to finish the job, and so we did in historic fashion.

The bottom of the eighth began harmlessly enough when Jon Burroughs, our centerfielder, flied out. Next, left-fielder Ryan Venter singled. That brought up our No. 8 hitter, Ricky Long, who proceeded to hit into what would normally have been a routine double play.

But there was nothing normal or routine about either Ricky or this game, as Ricky, who was "normally" our slowest runner, proved by beating out the relay to first. When someone asks me

208

to define hustle, I rewind the video I have embedded in my memory of Ricky plunging toward first and beating that throw. That's hustle.

And that, in a sense, was the game. A moment later, Evan McQuide, our No. 9 hitter, hit a single, which allowed Ricky to take second.

Then, following an intentional walk to Pat Hughes, our third baseman Ryan Sweeney rifled a single to right-center, and Ricky was triumphantly bounding home.

Cue pandemonium.

****

I was right: even though I coached one more season with the Eagles, that *was* the last championship game I would oversee for them.

Fortunately, there was another epochal championship game with another team in my future, but I didn't know that at the time.

In the meantime, the following fall, the fall of 2000, the various legal stratagems with which Jim Kelly had managed to stay the wrath of my superiors at BCHS—and *their* superiors in the school board—ran their course, and, depending on which metaphor you prefer a) the poison began to take effect, b) the sword of Damocles hanging over my head began to drop and/or c) the buzz saw aimed at my vitals began to buzz again.

I can joke about it now, but it certainly wasn't a laughing matter at the time!

Also, I expect you may differ with some of the decisions I made during my second bout with the powers that be—particularly my decision to ultimately refuse the district superintendent's offer to allow me to remain varsity coach provided I gave up my Mickey Mantle team. Certainly some of my supporters--including several of my staunchest friends—did.

However, dear reader, if you know me—and I expect that you do by now—you know that I didn't have much choice in the matter.

And, of course, neither did the still angry bureaucratic bees have much choice as they were only too happy to see me disappear from the scene.

Chronologically, this is how the last, traumatic year and a half of my star-crossed tenure as head coach of the Eagles played out. If the timeline leading up to my vanishing reads stroboscopically, in a way, that's how I experienced it, as well as how I remember that surreal final passage: as a series of serial, progressively numbing flashes:

July 1999. At the urging of the superintendent, the Bethlehem School District Board passes a resolution effectively presenting me with an ultimatum to either resign from Mickey Mantle or be dismissed as varsity baseball coach.

FLASH—

September 1999. Jim Kelly initiates a federal lawsuit against the Bethlehem school district, charging that the district had violated my first amendment rights of freedom of speech and freedom of association as well as my fourteenth amendment right to equal protection. Kelly notes—correctly—that there are over two dozen other Suburban Council coaches, including five in Bethlehem, who are also coaching out of season.

The suit asks for $1.75 million in damages. In a press release to the local media, which helps make the case a *cause célèbre,* I state that if the funds were ever recovered I would use them to build a baseball field with lights for the community.

FLASH—

February 2000. In the sole negotiating session with the district, I offer to drop my suit if the district will agree to cease interfering with my Mickey Mantle work, as well as assigning the assistant athletic director to oversee the baseball program. The superintendent rejects my offer and does not make a counteroffer.

FLASH—

October 2000. In the mail I receive eighty pages of legal discovery amassed by the district scoring my professional ethics. Also in the mail is a notarized copy of the Easton Sports Master Coach Award, a nationally recognized award given to an outstanding amateur coach.

FLASH—

November 2000. In a preliminary hearing, in which our side offers seven witnesses and Bethlehem offers none, Judge James MacAvoy dismisses my case. His fourteen-page decision states that a coach's speech is not of sufficient public importance to be protected, nor that the relationships on an athletic team are sufficiently "intimate" to require protection. Earlier I had rejected my attorney's request to use a private investigator in order to expose the other coaches who were breaking the Suburban Council rule. Consequently, I am not able to prove the equal protection complaint.

In an aside the judge notes that he personally fails to see the utility of the rule. He also commends me for my work with the community. This does not make me feel better.

FLASH—

November 2000. In a move I was half-expecting, the superintendent comes to my classroom and offers to allow me to continue as varsity coach if I will agree to resign from the Mickey Mantle team. I respectfully decline.

FLASH—

December 2000. At a public school board meeting in the same building where I "beat" the district six years before and was hired as Head Coach, where I am in attendance, I am formally removed as head coach.

211

The next day I call in sick for the first time in nearly twenty years.

Suddenly it was over. Fade to darkest black…

CHAPTER 12:
REDEMPTION

This spring has undoubtedly been special for the entire LaSalle community, but no matter what happens at Binghamton's NYSEG Stadium vs. Section I champion RC Ketchum, head coach Jesse Braverman has plenty to celebrate—win or lose.

—James Allen, *The Record,* June 3, 2005

Somewhere up there, I know that Sal is smiling.

—Pat Mulcahy, athletic director of LaSalle Institute, referring to the late Sal Fiorino, LaSalle's former varsity baseball coach, after the Cadets' historic 27 game victory run

AND things stayed dark for quite a long time.

Two years, two months, and fourteen days to be exact.

Mind, several good things happened during this period.

First, I started working at Hayner's Sports Barn, an indoor training facility in Halfmoon, New York, where I gave private lessons on hitting and pitching both to individuals and small groups. To say that this unassuming facility off Route 236 saved my life is only a slight exaggeration. On the surface, the Barn, which is owned by brothers Ken and Norm Hayner, was a place where I was able to continue my passion for coaching while interacting with students and other coaches from the Capital Region.

But beyond that it really was a sanctuary and a place where I could heal from the great loss and trauma I had suffered.

213

Second, through the miracle of Classmates.com, I got back in touch with my coauthor, Gordon F. Sander, who had been my Public School 131 classmate and occasional stickball opponent, and whom I had last seen in the vicinity of Jamaica High. Gordon, then a journalist living in London, coincidentally was about to move to Ithaca, New York to be artist in residence at Cornell University, which facilitated an in-person reunion.

Impressed with my story, as well as my palpable distress, Gordon urged me to write a book about my life, including my recent travails, as a kind of a therapeutic exercise.

"And if it's any good I will take a look at it and help you with it," he vowed.

Well, I guess it was, because here we are, aren't we?

The problem was that we didn't have an ending, at least at the time, or at least a satisfactory one.

No matter: I set to work, and a very helpful and therapeutic exercise it was. I found that I had a facility I wasn't aware of, or at least hadn't used very much since my formal education ended.

It also felt good.

The third thing that happened—or, more accurately, didn't happen—is that I didn't take my life.

I am only being partly facetious here. I could go into sordid detail here, but I won't. Suffice to say that at one point my wife was sufficiently worried about me to hide most of the contents of our medicine cabinet from me. Not that I ever actually visualized taking my life, but, despite the valiant efforts of my wife and friends to keep my spirits up, life had lost most of its meaning to me.

I also continued to work at the Sports Barn, as well as at the Rensselaer Polytechnic Institute in Troy as a volunteer assistant coach.

These things were all good and helpful.

Nevertheless the fact remained that I remained lodged in a deep psychological abyss. Ask any coach worth his or her salt who was unfortunate enough to have his or her team taken away, for one reason or another, and I am sure he or she would empathize.

214

One of those who stopped by the Sports Barn to offer encouragement to me during those trying obsidian days was Sal Forino, the head baseball coach at the La Salle Institute in Troy, New York.

Several weeks after that visit I learned, to my great distress, that Sal had died in an automobile accident.

****

FLASH FORWARD one month to February twenty-sixth, 2003. I am seated in the library of La Salle Institute in South Troy, being interviewed by a committee comprised of several faculty and coaches, a board member, a student-athlete, and a La Salle parent for the position of the school's varsity coach.

Needless to say, the path to that interview, and the decision to apply for Sal's job, which had been advertised locally, was not an easy one. As much as I was keen to coach again, this was not the way I had pictured it happening.

And yet upon reflection I was reasonably confident that Sal would have approved.

So there I was on that memorable winter's day a decade and a half ago being grilled by the late coach's colleagues as a possible candidate to replace him. First I offered my condolences for Sal's loss. I also mentioned the kind words of encouragement which Sal had extended to me when he stopped by the Sports Barn.

Duly noted.

Then the grilling began. As I expected, I was asked to explain the still painful circumstances surrounding my dismissal from Bethlehem. I stated to the committee that, despite the unfortunate manner with which my relationship with Bethlehem had ended, my actions throughout the affair, including and especially my work with the Mickey Mantle team had been positive, and not negative.

I stressed that I felt it was a good thing to do volunteer work for the community. Moreover, I noted, my service to Bethlehem was not by any means limited to the Mickey Mantle team. In fact,

I noted, I had donated comparatively more of my time and energy to the daily Jesse Ball pickup games I held during the spring and summer.

Duly noted.

Next came the inevitable question. "We heard that even after you lost the court case," one of the committee members asked, "you were told that you could continue as varsity coach if you would resign from the Mickey Mantle team and you refused. Why?"

My answer was, "In 1972 George McGovern lost every state in the Union except for Massachusetts and the District of Columbia. He even lost his home state of South Dakota.

Then a couple of years later, after Watergate, McGovern was asked about his landslide loss to Nixon. His reply then is the same as my reply now. "I'd rather lose the right way," he said, "than win the wrong way."

I wanted to express that my actions at Bethlehem were based on principle, and I sensed from the committee's non-verbal reaction that they understood. In any case, I sensed that the pendulum was swinging my way.

Finally, another member of the committee asked, "If we give you this job, where will you be five years from now?" Eight pairs of eyes were on me now.

"If you honor me by granting me this position," I said evenly, "five years from now I expect to be doing this job."

Well, I was correct. Five years later, I still had the job. Building on the foundations of the excellent program which my predecessor had bequeathed me, I managed to take the Cadets to a new level of success, notching winning records in my first two seasons as varsity coach.

In 2005, two years after I was hired, I had my greatest season to date. And so did La Salle. Together the Cadets and I fought our way through an arduous Big 10 title race, emerging with victories over Troy, Colonie, and Shenendehowa to secure the Class AA title. "The Braverman Redemption," James Allen, then of the *Troy Record,* now with the *Albany Times-Union,* called it. I wouldn't be so presumptuous as to say that I redeemed the Cadets. After all, they were pretty good to begin with.

But they certainly redeemed me. You might say that it was a mutual healing process--as well as a mutual learning one.

To be sure, the process of transitioning from a large suburban public high school to a medium-sized Catholic school centered around a strict leadership training program required a certain mental adjustment—or at least one would think so.

As it turned out, my transition to "the La Salle way" was quite smooth.

Of course, the leadership and religious components of the La Salle ethos and syllabus were new to me, but the values which the one hundred and fifty year old educational institution sought to inculcate its students with—honesty, commitment, diligence, trustworthiness, and loyalty—were not. It was true that La Salle and I had taken different paths to those values, but our final destinations were and remain remarkably similar. I might not have served in the military, as some of my new colleagues had; I may have been raised in the Jewish faith and not the Catholic one, but it soon became clear to me that La Salle and I were a superb, if somewhat incongruous match.

A match made in heaven? I'm not sure about that—but certainly a match made in baseball heaven.

****

THEN, three years later came the pinnacle, the 2008 season and the Cadet's history-making twenty-seven-game winning streak and that other even greater (if that is possible) championship.

That was certainly the pinnacle.

Sure enough, there was one more championship game to remember—as well as one more difficult loss to swallow.

I will defer to my co-author's description of that apotheosis he included in a feature he wrote about me and La Salle for *Hudson Valley* magazine:

217

On the evening of Saturday, June 7, 2008 a crowd of over 4,000 upstate baseball die-hards filled Troy's Bruno Stadium to watch the Section II Class AA championship game between the La Salle Cadets and the Columbia Blue Devils. The resultant nail-biter didn't end until 12:22 the next morning, when La Salle second baseman Will Remillard singled up the middle in the bottom of the seventh to send the winning run home—and the delirious Cadets, along with their exultant coach, Jesse Braverman, into the familiar, frenzied victory scrum on the mound.

The keyed up fans streaming into the night knew that they had seen one of the best baseball games of their lives. Few realized that they had also witnessed the culmination of one of the most impressive—and moving—comebacks in the annals of high school coaching...

Gordon's article, which moved Debbie and me to tears, continued:

The La Salle Cadets have learned a lot from Jesse both about baseball and about life. "I've learned to do my best no matter who is coaching," says center-fielder Scott Morrisey, "to do the best I can in whatever I try."

They've also learned that—contrary to what Vince Lombardi and all too many current coaches as well as parents believe—winning is not everything. It's how the game is played that counts. When asked to describe his fondest memory of the Cadets' epochal 2008 season, Scott quoted the pep talk Braverman gave the dejected team as they sat in a circle around him on the field after losing the final game of the season.

"He said that he wasn't disappointed that we had lost the game," Scott said.

"He said that either way, the season was coming to an end. Instead, he said, what was disappointing to him was that it was the end of the season, and that he would no longer have the privilege of working with us as a team anymore. That is something I think I will always remember."

218

"Somewhere up there," says Pat Mulcahy, La Salle's athletic director, *referring to Jesse's predecessor, the late Sal Forino, "I know that Sal is smiling."*

"Amen!"

In the meantime, I am pleased to report that I have had continued success with the Cadets. Perhaps we haven't had any more unbeaten runs, but we've done well.

In 2010, we won our sixth league championship in seven years and narrowly missed reaching the sectional finals. In 2011, we were hit hard by the loss of many talented players to graduation, three of whom would go on to professional careers. As enrollment declined, as it had with many private schools at the time, we had to rebuild instead of reload. Our efforts began to bear fruit just one year later, when in 2012, we once again qualified for postseason play.

In the meantime I continued to rejoice in the success of my former players who went on to play professional baseball, as well as to become coaches themselves. There have been ten such fortunate players, five from Bethlehem, and five from La Salle. I feel fortunate indeed to have crossed paths with such exceptional talent. The roll of honor from Bethlehem includes Cameron Smith (Detroit Tigers), Matt Quatraro (Tampa Bay Rays), Dan Conway (Colorado Rockies), Matt Elfeldt (Boston Red Sox), and Avi Rasowsky (Miami Marlins). From La Salle, there is Will Remillard (Chicago Cubs), David Roseboom (New York Mets), J.P. Sportman (Oakland Athletics), Patrick Reardon (Tampa Bay Rays), and Zach Remillard (Chicago White Sox).

Four of these, Roseboom, Sportman, and Will and Zach Remillard are still active in the minor leagues, but I am equally proud of the success the others have had off the field and believe their on-field experience helped develop the skills and character traits that breed success. And one of them, Matt Quatraro, has reached the zenith of baseball as the Assistant Hitting Coach of the Cleveland Indians. I suppose that Matt and I have come full circle in that I once coached him, and today, he is coaching me.

Every winter Matt comes to Troy and works with the Cadets on their hitting by providing a free hitting clinic.

At the same time, of course, I likewise continued to keep in touch and rejoice in the success of my special needs students, many if not most of whom have gone on to live rich and fulfilling lives as well.

Inevitably, several of my former special needs students continue to struggle. One of these is John, the student who ran away from class my first day of teaching at Bethlehem and in a sense never came back. John remains incarcerated today. He will be eligible for parole for the first time in 2018. Debbie and I continue to visit him every year, trying to give him hope and aid in his extended rehabilitation in whatever way we can. What can I say? I never give up.

Mike Jackson, my faithful scorekeeper, continues to live with the hardship of living with cerebral palsy. In early 2017 he suffered a heart attack from which it took a long time for him to recover. Nevertheless, he retains his upbeat attitude and personality. I have brought him to a few La Salle games when a minimal amount of walking is required, and he not only enjoys the games, but quickly learns the players' names and cheers them on with the same fervor with which he first exhibited when he began keeping score for the Bethlehem Lady Eagle basketball team thirty-five years ago.

I also continued teaching. In 2010, I began teaching at the Grapeville Christian School, an evangelical school in Climax, New York. My employer is actually the Greenville School District, since in New York State, if there are special needs students who attend a private school, the public school in that locale is required to provide Individualized Education Program (IEP) mandated services. I love working at Grapeville. Although my belief system differs from that of the school's we work well together. The students there are conscientious and upbeat, and the staff is a pleasure to work with.

Who would believe that a Jewish kid from Queens could become the baseball coach at a Catholic school and a special education teacher at an evangelical Christian school. Imagine that.

Meanwhile, I felt relaxed enough about the Cadets to take up acting again. Between 2011 and 2015, I had the privilege of appearing in regional productions of *Inherit the Wind*, *Rehearsal for Murder*, *Almost Maine*, *A Christmas Story*, and *Last of the Red Hot Lovers*.

In addition, I believe the range of life experiences I have had, both on and off the playing field, as well as in the classroom, and the range of emotions they have elicited have enhanced my ability to act and tackle more challenging roles. I recall my coauthor once telling me, "Before I write a novel, I think I should have a life first." I suspect the same is true, as least for me, for portraying a character on stage.

The rest of my life has continued to go well. My personal bench (to speak) is still very much in place. My marriage to Debbie is approaching three decades and remains as strong as ever. In 2007, Debbie underwent extensive heart valve replacement surgery. Unfortunately her mitral valve could not be repaired and a mechanical valve was inserted. Whether it be dealing with the aftereffects of her surgery, or other medical problems, Deb soldiers on courageously, and as always, remains by my side in good times and bad.

My brother Roger, who retired from teaching in 2004, has never lost touch with me. It may be true we have taken different paths in life, but we remain close nevertheless. He was there for me during my Bethlehem ordeal and Deb's heart surgery, and I was there for him during his recent hip replacement, as well as to share in the joy of his oldest grandson's Bar Mitzvah.

Bill Rappaport still occupies the front of my bench. Today Bill is an associate professor of Surgery at the University of Arizona and was recently Board certified in addiction medicine. I will always be grateful to him and my other friends for the support they showed during the difficult period following my dismissal.

****

ALSO, fifteen years after I was hired, I am pleased to say, I am still coaching at La Salle—although I didn't exactly plan it that way.

After the 2012 season, I was starting to feel the effects of "coaching burnout." The emotional wear and tear of making cuts and lineups, as well as dealing with disgruntled parents, was beginning to take its toll. I should insert that these side effects were mostly self-imposed, as the La Salle community, including players, parents, and the administration have always been supportive. Too, I was finally comfortable enough to be happy with teaching the game and no longer needed or wanted to be the head coach.

Consequently, in 2013 I switched places with my assistant coach. I thoroughly enjoyed my tenure as assistant coach. It was a joy to be able to focus solely on baseball skill development. I was able to contribute to the team's success without the burden of making difficult personnel decisions. The team won a league championship and one sectional game in 2013 and had winning records in 2014 and 2015.

In September, 2015, La Salle hired a new principal. In one of his first moves, he dismissed my former assistant as head baseball coach. This was an upsetting turn of events, to say the least. Upon returning from a vacation, I immediately met with the new principal and athletic director of one year in an attempt to save my colleague's position.

Unfortunately my effort to save his job was futile. Once this had been established, the principal and the athletic director surprised me by urging me to return as head coach of the La Salle varsity. My loyalty to my fellow coach was powerful and caused great internal conflict, but in the end, my loyalty to the current team and to La Salle won the day. There was no way I could walk away from the boys, no less turn my back on the school that gave me a new lease on life. Deep inside of me, I knew Joe would have approved.

Some other nice things happened. The standout event has to be the induction of both Joe Austin and I into The New York State Baseball Hall of Fame. This was a humbling honor to begin with, but to be honored at the same time as my mentor truly bowled me over. Among other inductees at the November 2015 ceremony were major leaguers Ken Singleton, Lee Mazilli, John Flaherty, Dennis Leonard, and Frank Viola.

The challenge of trying to speak on behalf of both Joe and I, and to express his legacy, was overwhelming, but I did my best. In the event, I borrowed from the key passage in my coauthor and my chapter about Joe in this book where we highlight the three words that we felt embodied Joe Austin's greatness: selflessness, commitment, and tolerance.

Going on to speak about my own career, I told the attentive audience that I have been frequently asked why I have coached so much and for so long. "My answer is really very simple," I said, "I coach to keep my coach alive."

In my two seasons since returning to the head coach position, La Salle has had a combined record of 33 – 9, with one league championship and two sectional victories.

Most importantly, my teams have learned how to play together, to always give their best effort, to lose gracefully and win humbly, and to love what they do. As for me, just about every day, whether I am on the field or off, in the deep recesses of my being, I can hear Joe: "Jesse Jimmy, you gotta live on the diamond."

Of course what Joe really meant in the larger sense, if I may be so bold to speak for him, is that you've got to live life full out. More than a half century after I first started running around Edison Oval to catch Joe's perfectly executed fungos, I'd like to think that I am doing just that.

INDEX